Climate Change

Is Racist

Climate Change

Is Racist

Race, Privilege and the
Struggle for Climate Justice

JEREMY WILLIAMS

ICON

Published in the UK in 2021 by Icon Books Ltd
Omnibus Business Centre, 39–41 North Road, London N7 9DP
email: info@iconbooks.com • www.iconbooks.com

Sold in the UK, Europe and Asia
by Faber & Faber Ltd, Bloomsbury House, 74–77 Great Russell Street,
London WC1B 3DA or their agents

Distributed in the UK, Europe and Asia
by Grantham Book Services, Trent Road, Grantham NG31 7XQ

Distributed in Australia and New Zealand
by Allen & Unwin Pty Ltd, PO Box 8500, 83 Alexander Street,
Crows Nest, NSW 2065

Distributed in South Africa
by Jonathan Ball, Office B4, The District, 41 Sir Lowry Road, Woodstock 7925

Distributed in India
by Penguin Books India, 7th Floor, Infinity Tower – C,
DLF Cyber City, Gurgaon 122002, Haryana

Distributed in the USA
by Publishers Group West, 1700 Fourth Street, Berkeley, CA 94710

Distributed in Canada
by Publishers Group Canada, 76 Stafford Street, Unit 300,
Toronto, Ontario M6J 2S1

ISBN: 978-178578-775-1

Typeset in Carre Noir by Marie Doherty

Printed and bound in Great Britain by Clays Ltd, Elcograf S.p.A

For Africa's youth strikers.
I hear you.

ABOUT THE AUTHOR

Jeremy Williams grew up in Madagascar and Kenya, and returned to Britain to study Journalism, International Relations and Cultural Studies. He now works as a freelance writer and activist, specialising in communicating sustainability to popular audiences. His blog, The Earthbound Report, has twice been recognised as Britain's leading green blog. He is the co-author of *The Economics of Arrival: Ideas for a Grown-up Economy* and editor of *Time to Act: A Resource Book from the Christians in Extinction Rebellion*.

For more information and extra resources
on *Climate Change Is Racist*, see:
www.earthbound.report/ccir

Contents

Foreword

There will undoubtedly be people who get stuck on the book title *Climate Change Is Racist*. But the undeniable truth is that climate change, as a global existential crisis, exacerbates racial inequality and racial injustice and it's vital that people understand how and why. The good news is that Jeremy Williams has taken on this task, clearly explaining the link between the climate crisis and systemic racism for those who may not have seen the connection.

The conversational style of Jeremy's writing will open the minds of even the most ardent denier of climate change and/or systemic racism. He helps us understand that climate change not only coexists with racism, but intersects with racial inequality. Everything we value as a necessity is susceptible to the impact of global warming – from water, food, health and wildlife to the economy, energy and transport, to name a few. Now consider the significant impact of systemic racial inequality, which already discriminates access to these vital resources on the basis of racial superiority. As I discuss in my own work, racism is a power construct created by White nations to benefit White people. It is fuelled by an unparalleled economic and political structure controlled by White nations, the by-product of which is White privilege – an advantage solely based on being White and not predicated on socioeconomic status, class or heritage. All of which denies Black and Ethnic minorities an equal value of life and liberty. This means that systemic racism will make the impact of climate change unequal. We will not all suffer climate change the same.

The United Nations calls climate change the defining issue of our time. This is true, because of how global warming impacts everything we value and depend on. However, the missing link here is that those who will first, and ultimately, pay the price for the devastating impact of climate change are those already bearing the brunt of racial inequality. This is why we cannot talk about climate justice without talking about racial justice. This includes the marginalised voices of women, particularly Black and Ethnic Minorities who face worsening inequalities because their lives and livelihoods are at risk.

Jeremy unpicks the potential failure of global nations to prepare for a global climate change catastrophe and shows why racism is a key component. The coronavirus pandemic took the world by storm in 2020 and caused the exacerbation of long-standing racial inequality, evidenced by high tolls of deaths from Black, Asian and Ethnic Minority communities in developed countries, which are apparently more industrialised and economically advanced. The impact of climate change will be a global catastrophe incomparable to any other urgent humanitarian crisis in recent history. Without drastic action to eradicate the roots of systemic racism, humanity is creating the blueprint for devastation and destruction of epic proportions. To prevent and fight this calamity, climate action must be inclusive of anti-racist action.

Hard work is necessary to deconstruct structural racial inequality as a global issue between White nations and Black/Brown nations and to understand the impact of the climate crisis in deepening long-standing structural inequalities between these nations, and between White and Black/Brown people within White nations. If there's one book that will help you to be an effective activist for climate justice, it is this one.

Dr Shola Mos-Shogbamimu
Lawyer, Political & Women's Rights Activist,
Author, *This Is Why I Resist*

Preface

My desk is made of scrap wood, in a makeshift office in the attic. This is as far as I can get from the lockdown home-school currently running at the dining table, and it is just about far enough to concentrate.

The last chapters of this book have been written under very different circumstances to the first, not just due to the challenges of a global pandemic. Events in America have catapulted racial justice up the agenda. When I started my research, there were relatively few people talking about climate and race. Today, I see articles making the connection on a regular basis.

The book turns out to be timely and urgent, though I almost didn't write it at all. I talked myself out of it, and then back in again. I wasn't sure if it was my book to write, but ultimately I had seen something I could not unsee. As I look out my attic window and reflect on my own story, I can almost pinpoint the moment I saw it first.

So this is what it feels like to be racially abused

Nairobi, 1998. I was seventeen, and attending a boarding school in Kijabe, Kenya. My friend Mark and I were in the capital for the weekend to watch the Safari Sevens international rugby tournament. We caught one of the city's notorious *matatus* – a vibrantly painted, riotously driven minibus. There's no schedule. It goes when it's full, and we crammed in and bunched up to let more passengers on board.

Half an hour later we could see the sports ground up ahead, and we left our seats and squeezed past other passengers to the door. The bus pulled in, a couple of others got off, and that's when the trouble started. The bus conductor, a young man in his twenties, wouldn't let us off the bus. 'No!' he shouted. 'Not you.'

'This is our stop,' I protested, but he reached out his hands and pushed me and my friend in the chest. We both stumbled backwards into the seats nearest the door. The bus moved on. A hundred yards later, we tried again at the next stop. Again we were pushed back down. 'You get off when I tell you to get off.'

The bus moved again, and now the conductor started to shout. His rant was partly directed at us, partly at the rest of the bus, sometimes at the world at large. My knowledge of Swahili was poor, but I knew enough to recognise mockery when I heard it. There was nervous laughter from the rest of the bus, but otherwise nobody said anything. Stop after stop he went on, pointing and gesticulating. We stopped asking to get off. We were silent, frozen. We were just going to have to sit this out.

The longer the conductor went on, the angrier he became. We seemed to have become the lightning rod for all this man's many grievances, and there was mounting violence in his eyes. At one point he leaned in and shouted right in our faces. I felt his spittle hit me, and I was too scared to wipe it off. I was convinced that a strike was coming.

It didn't. He shouted himself hoarse and finally fell quiet. He said nothing for several minutes, standing in the open doorway and staring out at the passing streets. Then the bus pulled in again, and he jerked his head at us. We got out. The bus was on a circular route, and we were right back where we had started.

Feeling rather shaken, we lined up for another bus.

The privilege of surprise

It wasn't the first time I had been harassed for being White, but in five years living in Kenya, it was the first time I had felt a genuine threat of violence. Whites were usually treated with post-colonial deference and an assumption that we were well off and well-connected. This kind of abuse was unexpected, and it caught me by surprise. The incident stands out because it was so unusual, and, with hindsight, I can recognise that surprise as a privilege. For many, being harassed on a bus *is* expected. It is unsurprising, perhaps even normal.

If you had asked me at seventeen, I would have told you that racism in 1990s Kenya was a reality. But I'd have said that I wasn't racist myself and that racism did not affect me. It was not a part of my world, I was not complicit, and that's why it was such a shock to be racially abused.

But of course, it was a part of my world. It's just that I was on the benefiting side of Kenya's racial inequality. Every other person on the bus would have scoffed at the idea that racism had nothing to do with me. Whether I was aware of it or not, whether I wanted it or not, I enjoyed the advantages of being

White. There are better ways of doing it than shouting at teen-agers, of course, but the conductor's actions on that day called out my privilege. I've often reflected on this. I don't condone his actions, but, with the benefit of time and distance, I am grateful for the lessons that emerged from the experience.

Difficult questions

I don't tell this story to demonstrate that I somehow understand racism – quite the opposite. I experienced a one-off incident of prejudice, and it opened my eyes to a systemic injustice that I had not seen. I've shared this story because the difference between racist actions and racist structures is vital to everything else that follows.

On reading the title of this book, many people will reflex-ively reject the idea. No, climate change isn't racist. How could it be? What's race got to do with it? Why do people always have to drag race into everything?

A different group of people will instinctively agree – of course climate change is racist. How could anyone not see that?

Whatever your response, I would invite you to read on with a spirit of enquiry. The book has certainly been written in that spirit, as an investigation into some difficult questions: Is climate change racist? If so, how and why? What can we do about it? I have not been satisfied with easy answers in writing it, and you deserve more than easy answers in the reading of it.

This book is going to strike a nerve for some readers. White privilege is a difficult thing to talk about, and I want to talk about it at the grandest possible scale. So, I want to say at the outset that it isn't about blame. As I will explain in the introduction, the racial dimension of climate change is much deeper than our individual perspectives or whether we consider ourselves to be racist or not. As a White man, I am implicated in an unjust system, but that does not make it my fault. Nobody should be shamed for the colour of their skin, whether they are advantaged or disadvantaged by it.

I should, however, be prepared to take some responsibility for the privilege I have inherited, and be proactive in redressing inequality. I cannot set myself apart from the injustice, as I did as a teenager in Africa. I am complicit in all of it. This is my problem too.

I will try as much as possible to speak for myself. I naturally use a collective 'we' in my writing, because I feel that it builds rapport. I also realise that it generalises unfairly, and I have avoided it in the book. Where it does occasionally appear, I am referring to you and I, reader and writer. I'll talk more about that and why it matters in Chapter 1.

This book has been spurred by two waves of protest. I was already researching the connections between climate and race when the Youth Strike for Climate movement and Extinction Rebellion broke through. A wave of energy ran through the climate debate and through my own project. Then in May 2020, George Floyd was killed by the police in Minneapolis, provoking mass demonstrations and a renewed call for racial justice. Much of the book was written at that point, and I felt myself swept up and carried along by events, challenged on a daily basis by the sense of urgency.

This has not been a comfortable book to write, neither in its contents nor the circumstances of its writing. It probably won't be a comfortable book to read either. I can't apologise for that, though I will try to keep it engaging and non-judgemental. I'll also try to keep it short. There are so many good books in the world, and I won't presume to keep you too long.

Introduction

On the next page is a map of per capita CO_2 emissions (Figure 1). It shows where in the world people have the highest carbon footprints. Darker shading shows the highest footprints, and therefore those who are most responsible for the breakdown of the climate. The lighter the colour, the less the citizens of that country are contributing to the crisis.

Figure 2 is a map of climate vulnerability. It shows those places that will suffer the most serious effects of heat, drought and sea level rise. Here, lighter shades indicate relative safety; darker shades show mounting risk. It is the darker shaded areas that could be considered the front lines of climate change.

Two different worlds

When presented side by side, these two maps are almost negative images of each other. In the first, there is a band of lower carbon footprints across the middle, with higher footprints on either side, and in the second the shades switch over. What this means is that there is a stark disconnect between the causes of climate change and its consequences. Those who are most responsible for damaging the atmosphere face much lower risks, while the greatest dangers fall on those who are least responsible. This is the injustice of climate change.

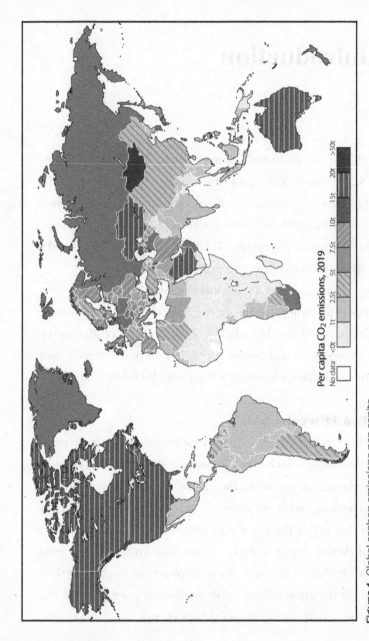

Figure 1. Global carbon emissions per capita.

Source: Our World in Data, based on the Global Carbon Project. Published under a Creative Commons Licence.

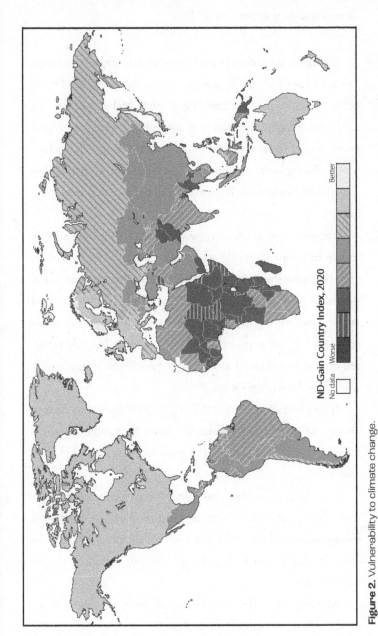

Figure 2. Vulnerability to climate change.

ND-GAIN Country Index, based on the University of Notre Dame Global Adaptation Index. Published under a Creative Commons Licence.

Take another look at those two maps and consider income. The countries with the biggest per capita footprints tend to be richer. That's no great surprise. People with higher incomes can afford more flights, more meat, more energy and more material goods, and thus their carbon footprints are larger. The richest have a disproportionate impact. Conversely, those with smaller disposable incomes use less energy and have a lower ecological impact.

Vulnerability is the inverse. The richest are more likely to live in temperate areas where the climate is less extreme, and they have the money to protect themselves. Britain experienced a heatwave recently, and one of my neighbours had an air conditioning unit fitted. The poorest cannot afford air conditioning, nor many other adaptations to a changing environment. When disaster strikes, they have fewer reserves with which to rebuild or relocate.

It's a generalisation, but the two maps suggest that climate change is predominantly caused by the richest and mainly suffered by the poorest. This is the economic injustice of climate change.

Now look at the map again, and this time consider race. In that top map, what skin colour do most people have in the most carbon intensive countries? With some exceptions, it is hard to escape the idea that climate change is mainly caused by people with fair skin.

Moving on to the second map, there is another mirror image: a band of climate vulnerability across the centre of the globe. It runs from the Caribbean and Central America, through Africa, and on to South Asia. Those most vulnerable to climate change are people of colour. This is the racial injustice of climate change.

Three kinds of racism

When people talk about racism, they often mean racial prejudice: the actions and opinions of racists. That is the most obvious kind, visible in the so-called 'casual' racism of elderly relatives, perhaps, or in the distinctly less casual actions of the far right. It's the racism of White supremacists, fascism and football hooligans. Those are the most shameless forms, though it's much more prevalent as a quiet bias, unexpressed and maybe even subconscious. Either way, this is individual racism, and it may be strong or weak, overt or internalised.

Climate change is not that kind of racist.

It's not a person. It doesn't have feelings or opinions. It is incapable of prejudice. But there are other kinds of racism.

A second form of racism is institutional racism. It's a term that rose to prominence in Britain through the Stephen Lawrence Inquiry in 1999. The police had mishandled the racially motivated murder of the young black teenager and failed to bring a prosecution. The inquiry concluded that the Metropolitan Police had a problem with institutional racism, which it defined as 'the collective failure of an organisation to provide an appropriate and professional service to people because of their colour, culture, or ethnic origin'.[1]

Institutional racism happens when a public body is structured in a way that disadvantages people of colour. It occurs in policing and the courts, but also in school admissions, job applications, access to loans, and a hundred other ways that affect people's everyday lives. To paraphrase an example from those who coined the term in the 1960s, when somebody throws stones at a black family's windows, that's individual racism. When that family can't get a mortgage to buy the house in the first place, that's institutional racism.[2]

Because it is buried away in the processes of the institution, this form of racism does not require deliberate intent. That makes it hard to address. In the Stephen Lawrence Inquiry, police chiefs were quick to assert that their officers were not racist, but that wasn't the point. As American sociologist Howard Winant writes: 'racism must be understood in terms of its consequences, not as a matter of intentions or beliefs'.[3]

Climate change is not an institution either. It is not this kind of racist.

What we're talking about here is structural racism: patterns of disadvantage that emerge from the overall functioning of the global system, often accumulated over centuries. This is inequality at its broadest and least visible, because it functions without perpetrators or intent, unfolding through the structures of the global economy.

Many White people are unaware of structural racism. It lies outside the most common definition of racism as personal prejudice, and they have never experienced it for themselves.

Structural racism

There are no universally agreed definitions of these different aspects of racism. What I'm calling structural racism is sometimes called systemic racism, though some theorists might distinguish between those two terms. For the purposes of this book, I'm going to refer to structural racism as the scaffolding of policies, institutions, cultures and norms that perpetuate and reinforce racial inequality.

Structural racism is not a bad habit that comes and goes, depending on whether the president is Black or White – or orange. It's built into the foundations of society, and the origins of the inequality may lie in decisions that were made long before we were born – decisions to invade or to occupy, policies around housing or employment, or the wording of a constitution.[4] A key feature of structural racism is that it is laid down over time. It is racism with deep roots.

There is, of course, some overlap between these manifestations of racism. The problem with structural racism is that the explicit prejudice may have occurred long ago. The policies that purposefully excluded people of colour may have been abolished, but they have a long echo. It might look like the problem is solved now that Black and White people can sit next to each other in Starbucks, but the long-term consequences of discrimination continue.

Advantages such as education or home ownership are passed on across generations. I have only been able to buy a house because my grandparents bought theirs in the 1960s. If my grandfather's surname was Wanyama instead of Williams, there's a good chance I'd still be renting.

Structural racism is embedded in the society we are born into. It can look like 'racism without racists', as the Puerto Rican sociologist Eduardo Bonilla-Silva puts it, because it does not need visible racists to perpetuate it.[5]

This is the way in which climate change is racist.

There is no committee of White people plotting to oppress Africa by disrupting the climate, but we can identify racism by its outcomes. The climate crisis will harm people of colour most, while they have contributed the least to the problem. The reasons for this are structural and historical. Later chapters will show how this came about, tracing the roots of climate injustice through slavery, colonialism and empire.

Because of these historical power imbalances, racism has already shaped the world's response to climate change. When action is delayed or when targets are weakened, it is the world's Black and Brown populations that suffer greater harm. Weak climate targets are racist policies. This is why the racial injustice of climate change can't be glossed over in order to avoid difficult conversations. If it remains invisible in the climate change debate, then racism will continue to shape responses to the climate emergency.

Today's civil rights challenge

If you click on your favourite news outlet and look for the latest on climate change, you are likely to find it under the 'environment' category. Politically, it usually comes under the remit of the environment minister. The big green organisations come to mind, with their iconic imagery of melting icebergs and polar bears. And yes, climate change is causing chaos in the natural world. But it's also a human crisis and a major justice issue.

As I hope I have demonstrated already, there is a huge racial dimension to climate change. That's not something that comes up very often in mainstream debate. There have been no bestselling books on the topic. It remains in the margins, in academic texts and in radical activist circles. A recent survey revealed that the majority of British people are unaware that climate change affects people of colour more – though a majority of Black respondents did know this.[6]

If we were to fast-forward 50 or 100 years, perhaps that will have changed. What will future generations say about those two maps at the top of the chapter? Will our grandchildren look back in disbelief at our attitudes, the way we look back at those who condoned or ignored slavery?

Activists from previous generations see a continuity between the struggles of the past and those of today. Gerald Durley is an African American pastor, now retired. In the 1960s he joined the campaign for civil rights, and was there in the crowd at the Lincoln Memorial when fellow reverend Dr Martin Luther King, Jr. made his famous speech. 'I never could have conceived of becoming a champion for climate change,' he writes. 'But, I have had a change of heart. Climate change is a civil rights issue.'[7]

If it's true that climate change is predominantly caused by White people, and disproportionately suffered by people of colour, then we are in the early stages of an epic racial atrocity, one that will echo through world history for centuries to come. Like the segregation that Durley and King opposed, it demands that we take a stand. What will our own role be? Will we silently go along with it, the way the silent complicity of previous generations enabled slavery, empire or Apartheid? Or will we throw our energies into the climate struggle?

The American journalist Wen Stephenson is a regular reporter on the front lines of climate activism. In his book, *What We're Fighting for Now Is Each Other*, he argues that climate change is a defining moral struggle: 'If the abolition of slavery was the great human, moral struggle of the 18th and 19th centuries, then climate justice is the great human, moral struggle of our own time.'[8] There is no neutral ground in the kind of moral struggle Stephenson describes. Everyone will have to decide where they stand.

Where are we going?

I am going to keep this book short, because I want as many people to read it as possible. So here's what you can expect. Chapters 1 and 2 look in detail at those two maps – first at who is causing climate change and how, and then at who is suffering the effects of climate change. Chapter 3 unpacks environmental justice within countries and across other environmental issues, such as pollution. We then look at some of the other injustices of climate change, beyond race, in Chapter 4.

Chapter 5 sets the historical context, showing the through line from slavery to empire to climate chaos. Chapter 6 explores climate change as violence, and draws links between climate change, police brutality and the Black Lives Matter movement. Chapter 7 investigates denial and silence, and introduces the idea of climate privilege. I describe compassion fatigue and the empathy gap in Chapter 8, before we turn to what can be done about it.

I'm afraid there are no easy solutions to the complex injustices addressed in this book, but neither are we powerless in the face of them. What you'll find in Chapters 9, 10 and 11 are three broad movements that can lead us towards constructive change. You can think of them as avenues down which solutions might be found. They are representation, restorative justice, and alliances and common cause. I close with what we can do as individuals in Chapter 12.

Then we're done here, and ready to begin.

1

Who causes climate change?

'We are fast approaching the point where our interference in the planet's great bio-geochemical cycles is threatening to endanger the Earth system itself ... We must begin to take responsibility for our actions at a planetary scale. Nature no longer runs the Earth. We do.'[1]

That's environmental writer Mark Lynas in his book *The God Species*, which describes how humans are now 'both the creators and destroyers of life'. Finding ourselves with God-like powers, 'we must use our technological mastery over nature to save the planet from ourselves'.

Or to pick another example, here is Stephen Emmott. His book *10 Billion* is 'about the unprecedented planetary emergency we've created ... Earth is home to millions of species. Just one dominates it. Us.'[2]

Who are we?

As a reader in Britain, I know what the authors above are getting at. I read these words in my own copies of the books, in my armchair, in my house with its fridge and its boiler. I hear cars outside and planes taking off from Luton Airport a mile or so away. When I read Emmott saying that 'we need to consume less', I know those words are directed at me as a Western consumer. (Indeed, both writers do specify at some point in their respective books who they're talking about.)

But let's imagine reading from a different point of view.

I grew up in Madagascar. It was one of the poorest countries in the world in the 1980s and 90s, and unfortunately it still is. If I were reading these words as a typical Malagasy person, I'd be doing so in a house made of mud bricks and a tin roof. There would be no car outside and probably no fridge – less than a quarter of households have a reliable source of electricity.

Average annual electricity use in Madagascar, per person, is 78 kilowatt hours (kwh) per year. Most people don't think in kilowatts, so let me put that into perspective. My fridge uses 1.5 kwh every 24 hours. I'm running the washing machine at the moment, which will use about 1.5 kwh, and I'll use around the same again to make dinner. In the warmer months of the year, my household uses around 4.5 kwh a day. Which means that every fortnight or so, my family uses more electricity than the average Malagasy person uses in a year.

However, my consumption is low for Britain, and Britain's consumption is low for a developed country. Let's look at a variety of other countries, showing electricity use in kwh per capita per year:[3]

- Canada – 14,612 kwh
- Kuwait – 14,090 kwh
- United States – 12,154 kwh
- Australia – 9,502 kwh
- Saudi Arabia – 9,407 kwh
- Japan – 7,150 kwh
- Germany – 6,306 kwh
- China – 4,617 kwh
- Britain – 4,496 kwh
- Madagascar – 78 kwh

How would a Malagasy person respond to reading that 'our interference' is disrupting the climate and that 'we need to take responsibility'?

There are only 27 countries with very high electricity use, of over 8,000 kwh a year. There are 30 or so countries with very low usage, below 150 kwh a year. Most countries sit somewhere in between, often at a level that could be met entirely with renewable energy and considered sustainable.

The top of the list is dominated by Northern European, North American and Middle Eastern countries, along with Australia and New Zealand. The bottom is almost entirely African countries. With the exception of oil-producing Middle Eastern countries where energy is cheap, there's a distinct colour divide here. Even the majority White countries that rank lowest for electricity use, places such as Moldova or Kosovo, still use 25 times more than most countries in Sub-Saharan Africa.

It isn't correct to say that 'we' are overconsuming. 'We' are not using too much energy. Some people are overconsuming. And most of those people are White.

Unequal carbon footprints

The amount of land needed to keep a modern consumer supplied with energy and resources is considerably greater than our literal footprint. As one energy commentator described it, if the average American consumed all their energy as food, they would eat as much as an Apatosaurus.[4] At 40 tonnes and 70 feet long, that's a footprint of an entirely different kind.

Let's broaden the scope from electricity to carbon, and consider the impact of these larger fossil footprints. Since energy use is the biggest component of carbon footprints, it is a similar picture: again we see a vast inequality between countries. Per capita carbon footprints in Madagascar are around 0.16 tonnes. The average Australian has a carbon footprint 100 times larger, at over seventeen tonnes of CO_2 per year.[5] So do citizens of the United States and Canada.

Many European countries come in at half that and could feel superior when comparing themselves to those across the Atlantic. But compared to footprints of those in Malawi or Rwanda, there is less to be smug about. China is also in this middle bracket.

As the map in the introduction showed, the world's biggest carbon emitters – on a per capita basis – are clustered in the Northern Hemisphere and the Middle East. The lowest footprints are in Sub-Saharan Africa and small island states. The South Asian countries of India, Bangladesh and Pakistan also have footprints below two tonnes per person per year.

The most obvious inequality here is economic. The poorest countries of the world have the lowest footprints. The highest footprints are in the highly industrialised North, and among the well-oiled nations of the Middle East. But if we only look at emissions at this particular moment in time, we will miss the wider perspective.

Historic responsibility

Average individual carbon footprints today show a wide discrepancy in responsibility. That becomes more stark when we look back through time. Some places have had a greenhouse gas problem for longer than others. Britain, for example, was early to industrialise and was by far the biggest emitter of greenhouse gases for over a century. With its coal-powered factories supplying the world with manufactured goods, Britain was more or less unchallenged as the world's biggest polluter from 1750 to 1900.

From that point on, the United States took over and remains the biggest total contributor to climate change today. At 399 billion tonnes of CO_2 to China's 200 billion, it is unlikely that China will catch up, despite the country's rush into coal in the early years of the 21st century (see Figure 3).

Looking at the cumulative totals by continent, we see that Europe, including Russia and the former countries of the USSR, is responsible for a third of all global CO_2 emissions.[6]

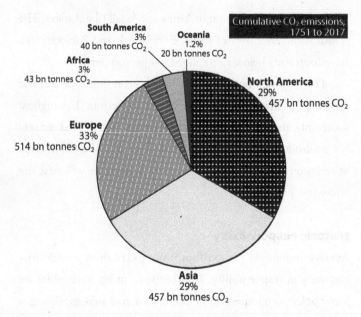

South America
3%
40 bn tonnes CO$_2$

Oceania
1.2%
20 bn tonnes CO$_2$

Cumulative CO$_2$ emissions,
1751 to 2017

Africa
3%
43 bn tonnes CO$_2$

North America
29%
457 bn tonnes CO$_2$

Europe
33%
514 bn tonnes CO$_2$

Asia
29%
457 bn tonnes CO$_2$

Figure 3. Who has contributed most to global CO$_2$? Cumulative carbon emissions from 1751 to 2017.

Calculated by Our World in Data, based on data from the Global Carbon Project and Carbon Dioxide Information Analysis Center. Published under a Creative Commons Licence.

North America adds a further 29 per cent, Oceania a further 1.2 per cent. All of these continents have had a majority White population during the period since industrialisation, which is what we are considering here with cumulative emissions.* Together they are responsible for 61 per cent of emissions.

---

* North America and Oceania were of course not White at all if you go back two centuries more; we will cover colonialism and conquest in Chapter 5.

Asia and the Middle East have contributed 29 per cent of total emissions, though this is spread over a larger population. The entire continents of South America and Africa have 3 per cent each. If we look at Africa more closely, we see that almost half the emissions are from South Africa. The contribution of most African countries is vanishingly small.

Countries are not ethnically homogenous, and we'll come on to that in the next chapter. It isn't always helpful to categorise entire countries by race, and it glosses over indigenous and migrant communities and their own particular stories. I am only really drawing generalisations here. Nevertheless, it is generally true that when we look at total responsibility for climate change, it has been disproportionately caused by light-skinned people of the Northern Hemisphere.

Climate change is a White problem.

That is, incidentally, why this is my book to write. White people like me need to take responsibility and cannot leave it to people of colour to make the case for racial equality.

Carbon corporations

Having said that climate change is a White problem, it would be very unfair to suggest that all White people are equally responsible. Racist structures persist because they benefit the powerful, so let me take another angle on this. The climate crisis is driven primarily by the extraction and burning of fossil fuels. While there are many fossil fuel customers, there are relatively few fossil fuel companies. Several studies have attempted to quantify the biggest offenders and publish estimates of corporate responsibility for climate change. They yield headline findings like these:

- Just 100 companies are responsible for 71 per cent of CO_2 (*Carbon Majors Report*, 2017)[7]
- 20 firms are behind a third of global emissions (the *Guardian*, 2019)[8]
- Almost two thirds of global warming since 1888 caused by 90 companies (*Climatic Change*, 2017)[9]

The exact breakdown depends on what time frame you use, but the point is clear. A small number of big companies have made enormous profits from activities that have destroyed the climate. Those companies all have a leadership and a CEO.

Jordan Engel is the cartographer behind The Decolonial Atlas, a radical mapping project in collaboration with indigenous communities. He took the 100 companies in the first of those studies above, looked up the CEOs and plotted them on a map.[10] CEOs change, but in 2017 the distribution of those CEOs was as follows.

Out of the 100 most polluting companies, 32 of the CEOs were in North America, nine of them in Texas alone. Eighteen were based in Europe and eleven in the Middle East. India had three, China four, and Indonesia's coal gave it five. Africa had eight of those 100 CEOs, three of them in South Africa. The whole of South America had five.

Again, these are proxy measures, but the power behind fossil fuels is tilted firmly towards the Northern Hemisphere. North America and Europe account for 17 per cent of the world's population, but they are home to 50 of the 100 biggest polluters. A Google image search suggested that 49 out of 50 of those CEOs were White (and one Latino). There was just one woman in 2017.*

The destruction of the atmosphere is signed off by men called Doug or Steve or Gary.

The polluter elite

Corporations and their CEOs are approximate too, not least because that list of 100 top polluters includes many nationalised entities. They represent governments rather than individual business interests. But we can expand the CEO idea outwards to look at the shareholders of the companies most responsible for climate change.

Dario Kenner is a researcher who studies the carbon footprints of the world's richest people and has identified what he calls 'the polluter elite'. This includes directors and investors in the most ecologically damaging companies. Their money finances ongoing climate change, and many of them use their political influence to promote fossil fuels and delay the transition

---

* This is a crude exercise, I know. It's not for me to assign a racial identity to people, and Google won't show if people have mixed race or Native American heritage, etc. But it would be odd if I didn't mention it.

to a sustainable future. Because people of colour are harmed by this delay, the lobbying of fossil fuel elites is racist.

Kenner used the same list of 100 companies from the Carbon Majors Database, filtered out the state-owned enterprises and began making a list of senior executives and directors.[11] Information on these shareholders is readily available, and listing them personalises what could otherwise come across as abstract power structures. Corporations, like markets, are ultimately just people. And in this case, they tend to be a certain kind of person.

'I actually looked up every single person in my database and so in a way got to know them,' Kenner told me. 'Almost all of them are older White males.'

Responsibility and justice

To return to where the chapter started, global responsibility for climate change is not equally shared. This fact is often neglected in discussions on the environment. I read a book recently that called for global governance, and it described 'a single machine made up of 8 billion humans' that was responsible for climate change.[12]

Or we could take the 2019 film *Planet of the Humans*, much talked about at the time of writing. Despite the planetary title, it barely sets foot outside of the United States. It concludes that 'we must accept that our human presence is already far beyond sustainability'. It ignores the differences in responsibility and makes one universal prescription: 'Less must be the new more.'[13]

You can tell me I have to live with less, but nobody should say it to the billion people who live on a couple of dollars a day. This kind of language obscures the injustice of our climate predicament.

So does the language of the 'Anthropocene' – the geological era in which humanity's actions are the defining feature of global change. By grouping everyone together in one universalist narrative, says the American geographer Kathryn Yusoff, the Anthropocene 'neatly erases histories of racism'.[14]

The language of environmentalism often reaches for inclusive terms in a well-meaning attempt at solidarity, aiming to create a global consciousness or unity of purpose. But campaigners should take care not to accidentally rewrite history in ways that serve a privileged minority.[15] Unity and solidarity are vital, but they are impossible without recognising that some parts of the world bear much greater responsibility for the climate emergency than others.

You'll notice that I use qualifying words such as 'predominately' and 'mostly' a lot. I don't really like them as words – especially 'disproportionately', which goes clanking like a freight train through any sentence I put it in. However, they're important because they avoid absolutes. The world doesn't fit into neat categories, and there are plenty of exceptions.

For instance, Africa has rich, privileged elites who can fly to New York to go shopping for handbags, and there are White Europeans who sleep behind the bus station. I know wealthy White men who live very responsibly. There are class structures and power imbalances that leave whole White communities voiceless. And there are forms of racism that this book won't investigate in detail, such as distinctive patterns of anti-Asian racism, China's actions in Africa, Islamophobia, or the Gulf States' attitudes to their imported workers from South Asia. Nuance matters, and it's wise to avoid blame and talk instead about degrees of responsibility.

With that in mind, what is the responsibility of the very poorest? The ecological footprints of the poorest 1 billion people – who are largely in Sub-Saharan Africa – are often well below the threshold for sustainability. There are other environmental problems associated with extreme poverty, but from a global climate change point of view they essentially bear no responsibility. Many of the world's citizens might think of climate change as something we are all implicated in and that calls us all to play our part. For those with the smallest footprints, however, climate change is something that is imposed upon them by others.

Constance Okollet, a farmer from Uganda, puts it this way: 'It was not until I went to a meeting about climate change that I heard it was not God, but the rich people in the West who are doing this to us.'[16]

2

Who suffers climate change?

Twenty-third of October 1984, the BBC screened a news report detailing the horrors of the Ethiopian famine. As Michael Buerk narrates from the refugee camp of Korem, clouds of smoke hang over hunched and skeletal bodies dressed in rags. These are horrific and powerful images. The Kenyan cameraman, Mohamed Amin, described how he wept in the edit suite over the footage of 'people dying as far as the eye can see'.[1]

The report moved the audience back at home on their sofas too, prompting a wave of charitable donations and a new interest in overseas development.

Three months later, Bob Geldof and Midge Ure's enduringly grating 'Do They Know It's Christmas?' would become the bestselling single of the year. It raised millions for famine relief as it urged listeners to remember those on the other side of the world where the rains don't fall, and to thank God it was happening to them and not to you.

Seventeen years later, a computer model ran at the Commonwealth Scientific and Industrial Research Organisation, Australia. The atmospheric scientists Leon Rotstayn and Ulrike

Lohmann were modelling the indirect effects of air pollution in Europe and the United States through the 20th century. Their findings suggested that industrial pollution in the Northern Hemisphere suppressed rainfall across the Sahel region. The model's predictions matched rainfall reductions in Ethiopia in the 1970s and 80s, and the way that the rains returned as Europe made progress on its air quality in the 1990s.[2]

It was a complex piece of research with lots of unanswered questions, and there are always many factors involved in a famine. But BBC News made the connection: 'Scientists in Australia and Canada say that pollution from Western countries may have caused the droughts which ravaged Africa's Sahel region in the seventies and eighties. Millions died in the droughts, which hit Ethiopia hardest in 1984.'[3]

Is it possible that, despite the outpouring of sympathy for Africa in the 80s, it was the Western nations that caused the problem in the first place?

Cause and effect

This story is about air pollution predominantly, but it illustrates one of the big complications of global environmental problems: the largest effects are often disconnected from the cause. Coal dust and industrial pollution from one part of the world can circle on air currents and disrupt rainfall patterns on another continent.

I can see plastic litter in the hedgerows near where I live and trace it directly back to the McDonald's drive-through on the retail park. But the carbon emissions from the cars queuing for the drive-through are different. So are the methane emissions from the beef production for their burgers. Those gases vent into the global atmosphere, vast and invisible. Who knows where the consequences fall?

The people who are most responsible for the climate crisis are not just less likely to be affected by it, but may not be aware of the effects at all. They might never even hear about them.

As outlined in Chapter 1, those with the greatest responsibility are disproportionately White countries of the global North. We now turn to an overview of climate vulnerability, and how that divides along racial lines. As will become clear, those most affected are disproportionately people of colour in the global South.

Second-hand smoke

The Earth's atmosphere is a thin protective layer around the planet. Looking out across a rolling landscape, it can be hard to imagine how human activity could disrupt something on a global scale. But as Bill McKibben points out, the world only seems big horizontally. If we look up vertically, 'the world is not nearly so large. Just a few miles above us – a couple of hours walk if we could walk straight up – you come to the end of the useful atmosphere.'[4]

All the world's greenhouse gases go into the same global atmosphere. Like children in a car with a parent who smokes, many are suffering from somebody else's pollution. The ecological harm is exported.

An Australian study into greenhouse gases and vulnerability found very unequal distribution of risk.[5] Several countries were ranked in the top fifth for carbon footprints but the lowest fifth for vulnerability. These were described as 'free riders'. These places 'are in a win-win position of achieving economic growth through fossil fuel use with few consequences from the resulting climate change'. The United States, China and most of Europe are in this category.

At the other end of the scale were 'forced riders': places that scored lowest for their carbon footprints and the highest for vulnerability. These are countries that are likely to 'suffer low economic growth and severe, negative climate change impacts'. Of the seventeen 'forced riders', seven were small island states and eight were countries in Africa. As the authors warn: 'this is an issue of environmental equity on a truly global scale'.

The sharp end

There are some obvious reasons why these 'forced riders' are at greater risk. Small island states are low-lying and easily overcome by rising seas. The Marshall Islands are made up of over a thousand atolls and islands, most of them no higher than five or six feet above sea level. The Marshallese poet Kathy Jetñil-Kijiner describes her homeland as looking like crumbs on a map – crumbs you might brush away with your hand.[6]

Such low-lying countries have contributed almost nothing to the global climate crisis, but will simply cease to exist if the current warming trend continues. Being small and remote, they carry little political or economic clout – which is why the US used the Marshall Islands as a nuclear test site in the 1940s and 50s. As the Marshall Islands' late climate negotiator Tony de Brum put it: 'We may be poor, we may be brown, we may be from remote Pacific islands that many struggle to find on a map – but we should not have been ignored six decades ago any more than we should be ignored today.'[7]

Countries do not need to be islands to be vulnerable to rising sea levels. Climate change will radically alter the geography of Bangladesh, making it one of most environmentally threatened countries.

Another factor in vulnerability is proximity to the equator. A warming world is naturally a more dangerous prospect in places that are already warm, though the big difference is whether you are rich or poor. Wealthier regions will pay to keep cool. Australia or Texas will be hotter, but they will spend more on air conditioning. Already, Dubai and Qatar, flush with oil money, even air condition outdoor spaces.[8]

Citizens of poorer countries will have to make do. In May 2017 a temperature of 53.7°C (128.66°F) was registered in Turbat, Pakistan. A handful of higher temperatures have been recorded on Earth, but only in deserts. Turbat is a small city, about the same size as Des Moines, Iowa – or Luton, England, where I live.

If it is hard to imagine how a city deals with such extremes, think of the coronavirus lockdown. Pakistani journalist Intikhab Hanif described how 'the city looked haunted' as everyone stayed at home, sleeping in front of their fans, as the electricity supply flickered in and out. Crowds came out as the sun went down, only for a dust storm to clear the streets again.[9]

The damage done

The non-governmental organisation Germanwatch compiles an annual report called the Global Climate Risk Index. It looks at climate-related disasters each year and ranks countries that have been most affected. The top ten for 2018 included both countries where I grew up.[10] Madagascar was hit by the one-two punch of cyclones Ava and Eliakim, echoing predictions that climate change leads to more intense tropical cyclones.[11] Kenya experienced twice the rainfall of a typical wet season. Rivers overflowed and floods affected 40 of the country's 47 counties.

The Global Climate Risk Index also has a cumulative list that shows which countries have been harmed the most over the last twenty years. This is important because it isn't modelling future climate change and predicting the unravelling as the world warms. This is damage already done.

The 2020 edition of the index covers the years from 1999 to 2018, and the worst affected country is Puerto Rico – courtesy of Hurricane Maria. It's the only entry in the top ten that is classified as a high-income country. Seven of the ten are lower-income countries, including Pakistan and Bangladesh, and two are classed as middle-income: Thailand and Dominica.

As Germanwatch points out: 'impacts from extreme weather events hit the poorest countries hardest'. They highlight two main reasons: those countries are more vulnerable in the first place, and they have fewer resources to cope with the disaster and rebuild afterwards.

The overlooked

The Risk Index is compiled using information from Munich Re, the German insurance giant. The United Nations (UN) warns that information about natural disasters, such as Munich Re's database, tends to skew towards the global North.[12] There is more detailed data capture, more precise figures on losses, and more scientists and statisticians paying attention. The result is that losses and damages are over-represented in richer countries.

This is amplified by the media, where the same problems apply. There are more journalists, photographers and TV news crews in richer countries. As we shall investigate later, people tend to be more invested in news stories about people like them. This can mean that disasters go under-reported in developing countries.

This over-representation of White suffering in natural disasters might explain a serious misunderstanding in the public imagination. In 2020, the relief agency Christian Aid ran a survey asking British people to say who they thought was most affected by the negative impacts of climate change. 26 per cent said it was Black, Asian or Arab people. 31 per cent thought White people were most affected, getting the injustice completely backwards.[13]

The relief agency CARE International compiled a list of the humanitarian disasters that received the least attention in 2019.[14] Heartbreakingly, there is Madagascar again – this time at number one. A drought across the country affected 2.9 million people, with almost a million needing emergency food aid, and yet this story attracted just 619 news articles in the global media over the course of the year. (In contrast, the Eurovision Song Contest generated 50,300 news articles in 2020.[15]) Scroll down the list and there is Kenya at number seven, this time for the drought that followed the floods. Of the ten under-reported crises, nine of them are in Africa. Almost all of them are climate-related, even where conflict is involved.

Here we see a particularly harsh aspect of climate injustice: many of the worst impacts of the climate crisis are unobserved. Those with the highest footprints don't see the damage in their own lives, and they might not see it in others' lives either. How closely do the polluter elite follow the news out of the Central African Republic or Chad? If people are unaware of the damage climate change is doing, is it any wonder that they struggle to believe that it is serious, or even happening at all?

This is exactly the same problem that the abolitionist movement faced when confronting slavery.

The slave trade happened on the other side of the world from the people who benefited from it. Most White British sugar or cotton consumers had never seen a slave or heard a depiction of a plantation. That was why Olaudah Equiano's autobiography was so powerful in 1789, as ordinary people finally heard from a slave first-hand.[16]

Western consumers today – who are majority White – are insulated from the effects of the climate emergency. They are also insulated from the news about the climate, and the stories that do break through are more likely to be about people like them. Black suffering goes unseen and unaddressed.

Undoing development

Thus far I have described observable trends and recent events. As we look into the future, it gets worse. Global heating will increase temperatures in places that are already hot. Rainfall will become erratic and intense, with greater risk of both floods and droughts. The latter can spiral into famine, displacement, political instability and conflict.

The number of people living in extreme poverty shrank by a billion between 1990 and 2015. But extreme poverty is officially defined as living on less than $1.90 a day, so most of those people still live very fragile lives. They may have managed to improve their lives through hard work, micro-loans or government programmes, but it doesn't take much to slip backwards. A lost harvest or a flood that washes away a home, and you're right back where you started.

Take the Indian state of Andhra Pradesh. Official statistics show that 2 per cent of people are lifted out of poverty every year, but the single figure doesn't tell the whole story. What is actually happening is that 14 per cent of the population are crossing the line out of poverty, while 12 per cent who weren't previously classified as poor cross the other way.[17] Life is precarious, and the path out of poverty is often two steps forward and one step back. Add a destabilising climate into that dynamic, and things get even more volatile.

'Unless the world takes bold action now,' warns the World Bank, 'a disastrously warming planet threatens to put prosperity out of reach of millions and roll back decades of development.'[18] And let's be clear: extreme poverty is concentrated in Sub-Saharan Africa and India. It is Black and Brown people who are being locked into poverty.

African action

Were the cameras to return to Ethiopia today, the location scouts would struggle to find the blighted landscapes that the BBC captured in 1984. They have been transformed. Ethiopia launched a comprehensive land restoration strategy to protect water sources and rebuild soils, using a mixture of modern technologies and traditional techniques. Huge reforestation programmes turned the land green and productive again. It is one of the most ambitious and successful land restoration projects in history.

Sustainability is at the heart of Ethiopia's national strategy. In 2013 it switched on what was then Africa's largest wind farm, and commissioned the continent's largest geothermal power scheme.[19] Addis Ababa has Sub-Saharan Africa's first urban light rail system. As a landlocked country it has to export through neighbouring Djibouti, and so it built Africa's first fully electri-fied cross-border railway to transport goods to port sustainably. The country's national plan, published in 2011, set a target for Ethiopia to become a carbon neutral middle-income country by 2025 – almost a decade before the phrase 'net zero target' became commonplace around the world.

I mention this because I have highlighted the effects of climate change on those in extreme poverty, but it would be a mistake to portray developing countries as passive in the face of climate disaster. One of the great under-reported stories of the climate age is the leadership of places such as Ethiopia. While there is more to do, over 30 African countries have made net zero commitments, more than any other continent.[20]

Having plundered Africa, former colonial powers have often re-cast themselves as saviours and benefactors through their aid programmes and relief efforts. But Africa is not waiting for the West to get its act together. If the worst of climate change is averted and Africa is spared disaster, it will not be because White people came to the rescue.

Who suffers?

As you will have noticed by now, Madagascar and Kenya are close to my heart and I keep highlighting Africa. But the racial injustices of climate change are observable wherever you live. Structural racism is a national as well as a global phenomenon, and its effects are much wider than climate change. We will look at those elements of environmental justice next.

To conclude this chapter: the effects of climate change are not evenly distributed. Suffering depends on wealth and geography. And as the sociologist Leon Sealey-Huggins writes, 'in most cases it is people of colour who will lose their lives as weather combines with inequality'.[21]

3

Environmental justice

'I had moments where I'm like, "It's not going to get this far; this is a waste of time, and my house isn't going to burn down." And of course it did burn down, and it was a shitty thing to live through.'[1]

That's the Hollywood actor Liam Hemsworth talking about losing his Malibu home in 2018. As wildfire spread through the California hills, the news reported a series of celebrities whose mansions had burned to the ground. It looked like a rare occasion where the world's richest and most privileged citizens were on the receiving end of a climate-related disaster. But California has its share of run-down neighbourhoods and trailer parks. Scratch the surface of that news story, and racial injustice is revealed.

A study from that same year found that 'wildfire vulnerability is spread unequally across race and ethnicity'. Some neighbourhoods get prioritised in brush clearing and have better coverage from the emergency services. People who own their homes are able to call on government support for rebuilding, while there is less help for renters. Sometimes simple things are forgotten:

in one case a few years before, the authorities neglected to send an emergency warning to the local Spanish radio station, and Latino farm workers didn't get the call to evacuate. A lot of these things divide down racial lines, resulting in 'census tracts that were majority Black, Hispanic or Native American experiencing circa 50 per cent greater vulnerability to wildfire'.[2] This class and race dimension is easily missed in news coverage that devotes more time to iconic landmarks or celebrity homes.

Dumping grounds

I've begun this chapter in the United States, as environmental justice has received more attention here than it has in Britain – though still nowhere near enough. It was civil rights campaigners in the US who first drew attention to the fact that ethnic minority communities often live closer to waste sites.[3] They face greater exposure to the pollution that comes from landfill, incinerators or toxic waste facilities and are more likely to suffer health complications as a result.[4]

Sometimes these neighbourhoods had been created through racial discrimination in housing, planning, lending or insurance arrangements in the first place. For example, the practice of 'redlining', where businesses would not provide mortgages or services to Black families in certain neighbourhoods, led to segregation and held down the value of Black family homes. Environmental injustice was piled upon social injustice.

As usual with structural racism, however, there doesn't need to be a deliberate intent behind the placing of dump sites.

Sometimes richer neighbourhoods had been able to deploy their resources and oppose a new development. Other times the reasons for the racial divide were buried away in the economics. Authorities needed somewhere to open a new dump, and looked for cheap land at the edge of town. Sociologist and activist Robert D. Bullard, often referred to as the father of environmental justice, puts it this way: 'These [polluting] industries have generally followed the path of least resistance, which has been to locate in economically poor and politically powerless African American communities.'[5]

With a source of pollution nearby, those who can afford to do so move away. House prices fall, which leads to people on lower incomes moving in – with a disproportionate number of Black and Hispanic families. What is sometimes described as 'White flight' occurs, ending with a demographic shift and the pollution concentrated in an ethnic minority neighbourhood.

Port Arthur in Texas is one such neighbourhood, where a predominantly African American community lives downwind of two refineries, five petro-chemical plants and an incinerator. Rates of respiratory illness and cancer are well above average. 'If one isn't flaring or smoking, another one is', says local resident Hilton Kelley. 'Sometimes it'll be really pungent, to the point where it stings the nose and eyes.'[6]

The problem is not unique to the United States, nor is it a uniquely racial phenomenon. A wide survey of environmental justice carried out in France found that towns with a high proportion of immigrants were more likely to have hazardous waste sites.[7] A survey across Eastern Europe found that Roma travellers are often restricted to sites located near landfills.[8] Mothiur Rahman, a lawyer and founder of Extinction Rebellion Muslims, told me how mosques in the UK are often on marginalised land and many are sited near pollution hotspots. The Poplar Mosque in Tower Hamlets, for example, has eight lanes of traffic outside on the approach to London's Blackwall Tunnel.*

Bomb trains

Port Arthur is doubly disadvantaged. As well as the pollution, it was hit hard by Hurricane Rita, and the nearby Highway 87 is so prone to storm damage that it has been abandoned. The area suffers both from climate change and the fossil fuel infrastructure that causes it.

This is another aspect of climate justice, and arguably a better documented one. All around the world, people are put at risk by the colossal forces of the fossil fuel industry.

One example in the US and Canada is proximity to railway lines that run oil trains. With the growth in fracking and mining tar sands, there are a lot more of these trains than there used to be, and when they crash they explode. The worst incident was the Lac-Mégantic disaster, where 47 people died when a train derailed in the middle of a small Canadian town.[9]

---

* I am not aware of any studies on this, but potential environmental justice issues deserve investigation – especially following the coronavirus pandemic and its unequal impact on minorities.

Analysis of the 'blast zones' either side of railway tracks reveals an unequal distribution of risk. Take Harrisburg, Pennsylvania, for example. Its population is 86 per cent White, but if you look at residents living within the blast zone, 38 per cent are people of colour.[10] This pattern is repeated along the tracks, and it has proved to be a rallying point for activism. Environmental activists found common cause with Black Lives Matter, and dozens of cities have participated in coordinated protests to stop oil trains.[11] These were high-profile acts of civil disobedience against fossil fuel companies that went on to inspire movements such as Extinction Rebellion.

Standing Rock

Pipelines have been another area for action, including the iconic protest at Standing Rock. This too had a strong racial angle, this time involving Native American communities. There is a long and tragic history of using land ownership and land value to oppress and displace Native American communities. One of the more recent chapters is over the Dakota Access Pipeline.

The Dakota Access Pipeline, or DAPL, was planned to link the Bakken oil fields with processing facilities in Illinois. The original route took the pipeline near to the town of Bismarck, North Dakota, but this was ruled out because it could compromise the town's drinking water. It was rerouted to cross underneath Lake Oahe, despite the fact that this was the source of drinking water for the Standing Rock Sioux tribe.

For historian and activist LaDonna Brave Bull Allard, who hosted a protest camp on her land, it was a clear case of discrimination. 'The Dakota Access Pipeline was rerouted from north of Bismarck, a mostly White community, out of concerns for their drinking water, but then redirected to ours. They consider our community expendable.'[12]

In 2016 the project was delayed for further environmental review and to investigate rerouting, and President Obama said he was monitoring the situation. Two months later and just four days into his term of office, President Trump overturned the delay. The pipeline was subsequently completed and opened, though a series of court rulings in 2020 decreed that proper environmental checks had not been carried out, the project should not have been allowed, and the pipeline ought to be drained and closed.[13] Appeals are in process, as eyes turn to President Biden. As long as the legal and political wrangling continues, half a million barrels of oil a day flow under the Lakota Sioux's drinking water supply.

Sacrifice zones

In her book *This Changes Everything*, Naomi Klein provides a term for this outsourcing of risk onto marginalised communities: sacrifice zones. She argues that the economy has always needed 'elsewheres' that could host waste sites, dangerous industries or ugly extractive operations – areas populated by 'whole subsets of humanity categorised as less than fully human, which made their poisoning in the name of progress somehow acceptable'.[14]

Sometimes these sacrifice zones are local, the 'other side of the tracks'. In a global economy, they could be anywhere.

One of the most scandalous examples is the Trafigura incident in 2006. The London-based Trafigura trading company bought a supply of heavily contaminated oil at a knockdown price, and refined it with a process that left them with a ship full of highly toxic 'slops'. Dealing with it responsibly was expensive, so they sailed the ship to Côte d'Ivoire and paid a local firm with no experience of toxic waste to take it away. It was dumped on an open landfill site, triggering a medical emergency that affected 100,000 people.[15]

There is no evidence that Trafigura's agents were being deliberately racist when they delivered their boatload of poison to Abidjan. It was just that Côte d'Ivoire was far away, cheap, with port officials willing to look the other way – and the people there just happened to be Black.

More recently, celebrity chef and activist Hugh Fearnley-Whittingstall climbed over a landfill site in Malaysia and found waste that had come from Britain.[16] It highlighted a problem that few were discussing – recycling was being dumped in developing countries. Britain, and many other developed countries, were accustomed to shipping their recycling to China. In 2017 China announced that it would no longer accept waste imports, and global waste supply chains were thrown into disarray. Waste started turning up in Malaysia or Thailand, until they quickly brought in bans of their own.

For some, the damage was already done. Phayao Charoonwong, a potato farmer in the village of Kok Hua Khao, can no longer grow crops or drink the water from her well. 'You are selfish', she says of the people who produced the rubbish on the other side of the world. 'Don't push the trash out of your country. It's your trash and you know it's toxic. Why do you dump your trash in Thailand?'[17]

Left behind

Communities in poorer neighbourhoods consistently face greater environmental risk. When disaster inevitably strikes, there is less support for recovery. The most notorious example of this was Hurricane Katrina in 2005. The poorest communities were already without protection, on the wrong side of the levees and facing the full wrath of the storm. 'The mayor wanted people to evacuate, but a lot of us couldn't evacuate,' said Renee Martin, an African American nursing assistant from Eastern New Orleans. 'I mean, everybody don't own a car.' No assistance was provided, leaving people to fend for themselves. Federal aid agencies were slow to respond after the storm, with marked differences between majority White and Black neighbourhoods. 'It's a racist thing,' says Martin. 'All of us was overlooked.'[18]

The discrimination continued long after the initial disaster, through the dissemination of government aid and grants, bank loans and rebuilding programmes. Fifteen years later, some parts of New Orleans have never been rebuilt and population numbers haven't recovered. Where districts were rebuilt, they also gentrified, pushing out the original residents in favour of (often White) incomers.[19]

This racial injustice is reflected in the altered demographics of the city. The population has halved since Katrina, and it is Black residents that have been pushed out. Unable to return and rebuild, over ten times more Black residents have left the city than White residents.[20]

The environmental justice lessons from Katrina have not been learned. When Hurricane Irma hit Miami in 2017, poorer neighbourhoods suffered most. The Black community of Liberty City, location of the Oscar-winning film *Moonlight*, suffered a triple injustice. Their city was more vulnerable to storm damage, received less support in recovery, and was then used as a dumping ground. City authorities located a landfill site for hurricane debris next to a residential area, and health problems, odour complaints and vermin infestations came with it.[21]

Is it racism?

Environmental racism doesn't need to be as dramatic as bomb trains and pipelines. It's usually much more prosaic than that. It might be something as ordinary as the air you breathe. A study of air quality found that Black Americans were exposed to 30 per cent more air pollution from transport than White Americans.[22] Or it could be the higher likelihood of exposure to lead paint or asbestos in your home or your school.[23]

Neither is environmental justice all about hazard. As Robert D. Bullard reminds us: 'Communities of colour don't get a fair share of the good stuff – parks, green spaces, nature trails, good schools, farmers markets, good stores. They get less of all the things that make communities healthy and get more of their fair share of the bad stuff.'[24]

These inequalities make people more vulnerable to shock, whether that is climate-related or a pandemic. The Bronx in New York was a hotspot of the coronavirus, resulting in more Black and ethnic minority deaths. A virus cannot be racist any more than a carbon particle can, but an underlying structural racism creates an outcome that divides along racial lines.

'When we talk about environmental racism, we're talking about illegal dumping,' says Congresswoman Alexandria Ocasio-Cortez, who represents the Bronx. 'We're talking about concentrating waste sites and concentrating highways and trucking zones through the poorest communities in the country, and the blackest communities and the brownest communities. And so, we already have an issue of extreme and acute concentration of respiratory illnesses in the Bronx.'[25]

Looked at superficially, it might seem as if many of these things are more to do with poverty than racism, and the next chapter will investigate how various forms of inequality intersect. But as we have seen already, structural racism does not require racist intent. Whether environmental injustices are perceived as racist depends in part on our perspective. The Puerto Rican sociologist Eduardo Bonilla-Silva suggests that 'whereas for most Whites racism is prejudice, for most people of colour racism is systemic or institutionalised'.[26]

It might not be possible to detect a racial prejudice behind many cases of environmental injustice. But if the end result is that people of colour are disadvantaged or disenfranchised, then we are talking about a racist structure.

American race scholar Ibram X. Kendi argues that racism has always worked this way. Throughout history, 'the source of racist ideas was not ignorance and hate, but self-interest'.[27] It's not that people hate those that are different and set out to oppress them. More often, the powerful act to benefit themselves at the expense of others. These racist policies are then legitimised with racist ideas.

In the case of environmental racism, White interests act to protect themselves from pollution and risk, creating racial inequalities. This inequality is then justified with racist ideas about the value of Black neighbourhoods.

In this chapter we have stepped away from global climate change in order to look at other forms of pollution, sometimes quite local. These examples help to demonstrate how structural racism manifests itself, and how minority ethnic communities often find themselves carrying a greater burden of risk and inconvenience, sometimes fatally so. This disadvantage springs from existing patterns of inequality and privilege, making environmental justice impossible to tease apart from other injustices – but no less significant for it.

Climate change is part of this complex interplay of inequalities, but on a much larger scale, writing its injustice over the globe and over centuries.

Climate change at the intersection

I am working on this chapter while the rest of my family is busy with home school at the kitchen table. Coronavirus has the country on lockdown, and my wife is cajoling the children through their English and maths.

The education children get while on lockdown can take very different paths. I know one family whose children are at an elite school where every pupil is expected to sit down to video lessons at 9am, wearing their uniforms. There are families like us who are somewhere in the middle – making do with downloads and weekly plans from the teacher, and exchanging music or drama lessons with talented friends. And I know a family on our street where, despite the best efforts of helpful neighbours, it's been nothing but television and trampoline for six weeks. The mother works, the father is at home with their only child and a heap of resources he can't make head nor tail of. Formal learning has paused entirely.

This is a live example of how inequality rolls on like a repeating pattern. The kids who are going to come out best from the lockdown will be the ones with educated parents in a stable relationship, a garden to run around in and a home full of books and games. For children with learning difficulties, an unstable home environment, or simply less access to learning resources, it could be a different story. If you had a good childhood when the crisis began, you have a good chance of emerging unscathed. If you were struggling to keep up at the start, you'll be further behind by the end.

The coronavirus crisis piles stress upon stress, poverty on top of poverty, and that's how inequality always seems to operate.

Patterns of (dis)advantage

I write as a paragon of privilege. I am White, male, heterosexual, cisgender. I am psychologically and physically normative, and a British citizen. I tick all the boxes, though one of the privileges I value the most is one that doesn't get mentioned very often: I speak English as my first language. It gives me access to millions of books and I can consult vast reserves of global expertise. Over half the internet is accessible to me. If I only spoke Malagasy, the internet would be a very precise 147,500 times smaller.*

These privileges are overlapping and self-reinforcing. It's perfectly possible for someone like me to end up shipwrecked

---

* According to live monitoring by W3Techs, right now 59 per cent of the world's web content is in English. 0.0004 per cent is in Malagasy.

of course, through my own doing or circumstances beyond my control. But the odds are in my favour, and there is only so far I can sink.

Imagine rolling dice in a board game. For someone like me, that tumbling cube isn't numbered from one to six. It's numbered from three to nine.

Now let's consider Grace Biswas, a lower-caste widow in the slum area of Dharavi, Mumbai. The opportunities open to Grace are very limited. She will find it hard to secure work or get a loan. Her only options may be jobs that nobody else wants to do, as a waste picker or perhaps emptying pit latrines. The stigma attached to these jobs would push her further to the margins. She may be a victim of violence, and if she is, her case may not be taken seriously by the police or the courts.[1]

The disadvantages she faces are also overlapping and self-reinforcing. She may escape poverty and live a full and satisfying life, but the chances are vanishingly small. When Grace rolls the dice, it isn't numbered from one to six either. The options go from two to minus four.

The injustice of climate change is no different. If you are already at a disadvantage – whether that is because of your race, gender, tribe or economic circumstances – you are likely to be hit harder by the climate emergency.

Standing in the way

In the first volume of her autobiography, *I Know Why the Caged Bird Sings*, Maya Angelou describes how young Black women are caught in a 'crossfire' of masculine prejudice and racial prejudice. Writing in the 1960s, she recognised that women of colour such as herself faced a unique combination of challenges.[2]

Intersectionality is an increasingly common term for describing these overlapping patterns of disadvantage. It's a word that has escaped its origins in theory and become something of a buzzword, though the first time I heard it I thought it sounded clunky and academic. That's because I'm a speaker of British English. Bearing in mind that Americans call junctions intersections, it's a more intuitive term than I first realised. Intersectionality suggests that if you're standing on the crossroads, you can get hit from two directions.

The metaphor was first used in 1989 by Kimberlé Crenshaw, a law professor and civil rights activist.[3] It came to her when reading about a woman who had brought a case of discrimination to the courts. She felt she had been overlooked for a job because she was an African American woman. The judge ruled that the company had employed women before, and it had employed African Americans before. It therefore could not be said to be biased. The judge didn't recognise that the discrimination might occur in the combination of those two identity categories.

Being 'both Black and female', says Crenshaw, 'she was positioned precisely where those roads overlapped, experiencing the simultaneous impact of the company's gender and race traffic'. The judge was like a first responder who would only treat her 'if it can be shown that she was harmed on the race road or on the gender road but not where those roads intersected'.[4]

Discrimination at work might happen at the intersection of race and gender. The chances of being affected by climate change lie on that same axis.

The feminist dimension

Women are disproportionately affected by climate change. The reasons are a complex tangle of pre-existing inequalities, including the fact that they are at an economic disadvantage. They receive lower pay, work informal jobs and/or are busy with care. This, in turn, reflects inequalities of power.

When poverty is measured by household, it can obscure the power dynamics at work in a family.[5] For example, while the split between men and women living in extreme poverty is roughly 50/50, women are more likely to go without food.[6] Men and children eat first. When climate change brings drought and hunger, women are more likely to go without.

Education, too, is often prioritised for boys when a choice has to be made. A family crisis such as divorce or bereavement can also be very different for men and women. Women may be left to care for children, or find it harder to find work afterwards. They are more likely to lose assets, including land.

Globally, there are elements of climate change that will quite specifically be more of a burden for women. In four out of five households without running water, women and girls do the water-carrying.[7] Drought or erratic rainfall caused by climate change will directly mean more work for women and girls.

Agriculture is similar. In many traditional cultures, men will seek paid work while women grow food and tend to household tasks. Many developing countries have more women farmers than men, which makes women more likely to be affected by harvest losses, drought and natural disasters.

Some research even shows that when disaster strikes, women are more likely to be killed in a natural disaster or flood. Again, the reasons are complicated – they may not have a role in decision-making about risk, so their specific concerns go unaddressed. That may include responsibilities to care for children or elderly relatives in an emergency situation, for example. In some places it may be as simple as girls not being taught how to swim. The more unequal women's roles are in a society, the more pronounced this burden of risk becomes.[8]

To flip the problem around, however: creating equality for women will also be vitally important to addressing climate change. Project Drawdown, a major international study, placed both family planning and education for girls in the top ten most effective solutions for reversing climate change.[9] The saying that 'women hold up half the sky' may be true in some unexpected ways.

Climate injustices

Climate change is an environmental issue, a race issue and a women's issue. And it's more than that. Climate change intersects with multiple dimensions of disadvantage. It acts as a multiplier of exclusion. I mentioned economic inequalities in the introduction and racial inequalities in Chapters 1 and 2. But anywhere that people experience marginalisation, climate change is likely to make it worse:

Indigenous people groups

Global heating is concentrated at the poles, so the indigenous peoples of the Arctic have experienced dramatic changes already. This threatens their livelihoods, culture and identity. 'Those who have traditionally lived closest to the land, and who today maintain the strongest connections to nature, are now at risk of becoming just a footnote in the history of globalization,' writes Inuit activist Sheila Watt-Cloutier in her aptly titled autobiography *The Right to Be Cold*. 'As our ice and lands are being lost to melting, rising shores, and severe weather, the traditional knowledge of our lands and environment that has sustained us for millennia has come under threat. Our very cultures are now at risk of melting away.'[10]

Coastal communities

Britain's coastal communities are among the most economically deprived in the country. The fishing industry has slowly eroded over decades, with no replacement for the jobs lost. Unemployment levels are high and poverty is persistent. Climate change will compound this marginalisation, as storms hit local infrastructure and erode coastlines.[11] Similar patterns are found around the world, as rising sea levels threaten those living nearest to the shore.

Nomadic tribes

Because they do not own the land they roam across, nomadic people groups are often disenfranchised and displaced. They already exist on the margins of society, and climate change risks their whole way of life. 'The lake and rivers we rely on for our drinking water – and to care for our animals – keep getting drier and shallower,' writes Ekai Nabenyo from Turkana County, Kenya. 'Droughts and famines have resulted in death to our animals as well as disappearance of livestock watering holes that have served my people for ages. As a result, our jobs as herders are in peril and our life generally has become one of a struggle for survival.'[12]

Children

The school strikes, inspired by Greta Thunberg, have propelled inter-generational injustice onto the agenda. More and more young people are realising that decisions made now will affect their long-term future, and yet they have no political voice. 'The strikes have given purpose and community to me and the many young people who felt powerless in the face of this manmade catastrophe,' says British school striker Francesca Laven. 'Young people do not have money to spend. We have no platform from which to speak. We cannot vote. By refusing to attend school, we exert the only power we have.'[13]

The elderly

At the same time, older people are also more vulnerable to climate shock. Heatwaves are the deadliest natural disasters in developed countries by some distance. We don't recognise them as such because of who the victims are, suggests Eric Klinenberg in his book about the 1995 Chicago heatwave: 'Heatwaves receive little public attention not only because they fail to generate the massive property damage and fantastic images produced by other weather-related disasters, but also because their victims are primarily social outcasts – the elderly, the poor, and the isolated – from whom we customarily turn away.'[14]

Health inequalities

COVID-19 presented a greater risk to those with underlying health conditions, and the same is true of climate change. Some may be less able to evacuate quickly in the case of disaster and find themselves in harm's way. Some may depend on specialist treatments which could be interrupted by floods or by power outages. An existing medical condition, such as asthma, can also make people more vulnerable. The *Medical Journal of Australia* reported that, during the 2020 bushfire crisis, 12 times more people died from the smoke and air pollution than from the fires themselves.[15]

LGBTQ

Climate change increases the burden on any sector of society that is already marginalised. As the queer activist and climate podcaster Peterson Toscano explained to me, this affects LGBTQ people in some specific ways. For example, LGBTQ people are more likely to experience homelessness, especially young people. That puts them at greater risk of extreme weather. When disaster strikes, they are often excluded from traditional support networks, including religious groups and in some cases their own families. This is at its worst in parts of the world where gay or trans people have fewer rights.

The unborn

Finally, to step back and think of climate change in a broader historical context: those most disadvantaged may not exist yet. It can be hard to account for the views of theoretical future people, though it is not impossible. The government of Wales proved that with their Wellbeing of Future Generations Act in 2015, becoming the first country in the world to secure the welfare of future citizens in law.[16] Many indigenous people groups have understood the importance of being 'good ancestors', but the English-speaking world has lacked the political language for this kind of thinking.

Poverty or race?

How about both and more besides. None of us can be reduced to a single issue. A human life cannot be explained in simple binary categories. The racial injustice or the gender injustice of climate change cannot be isolated from economics or from geography.

Neither can they be stacked in a hierarchy, as if one injustice is more important the others. It might be tempting to say 'the real issue is poverty' – it would certainly be easier from a political point of view. But where did the poverty come from? Enduring economic disadvantage can't be prised apart from current and historical racial divides. And history is what we have to look at next.

5

The deep roots of climate injustice

Where does the story of climate change start? If I take greenhouse gas emissions to be Exhibit A, then fossil fuels are the culprit and the story is a straightforward one. Trace the emissions backwards through history to the birth of the Industrial Revolution, and there are the origins of the climate crisis: James Watt and his coal-powered steam engines running mills and looms and water pumps.

Some might start later. The most famous graph in climate science is the Keeling Curve, showing the rise of CO_2 emissions at the Mauna Loa Observatory in Hawaii. It's the earliest annual record of CO_2 concentrations, beginning in 1958, and sets a starting point for the awareness of climate change if not the problem itself. Others would go back much further, arguing that human experiments with the atmosphere began with the forest clearances at the dawn of settled agriculture.[1]

Those approaches are based in the science of the greenhouse effect. A climate justice lens might tell a different story:

'We love to tell ourselves that it all started with the Industrial Revolution,' writes climate justice essayist Mary Annaïse Heglar. 'But we're telling ourselves a lie. It started with conquest, genocides, slavery and colonialism. That is the moment when White men's relationship with living things became extractive and disharmonious. Everything was for the taking; everything was for sale.'[2]

So far we have looked at who has caused the climate crisis and who suffers most from it, and how environmental justice intersects with other inequalities. I described how climate justice cannot be separated from other overlapping injustices. It cannot be separated from its historical context either, and that's the subject of this chapter.

The racism of slavery

1807, and the House of Commons is debating the Slave Trade Abolition Bill, again. It is the twelfth time such a bill has been proposed in the last fifteen years. The debate has raged for decades. Every argument has been heard, and in a matter of weeks the bill will be signed.

If the many years of debate had led Parliament to a greater understanding of human equality, there is little evidence of it here. Black lives are a commodity and referred to as such, with members talking about imports of 'fresh negroes'. The finer points of the bill are discussed – as one minister reminds them, it is 'not the intention of the house to abolish slavery, but the slave trade'.

This is important. Just ending the trade itself should inspire plantation owners to take better care of the slaves they already have, without depriving them of labour or giving the slaves big ideas. 'Be aware of propagating notions of political right among a people so unintelligent and so easily provoked to revolt as the negroes,' warns one MP.[3]

The institutions of slavery rely on a justifying ideology of racial superiority. For the defenders of slavery, black-skinned people were considered to be at best simple-minded and child-like, at worst barbaric. They were lazy and unproductive, and incapable of governing themselves. It really was for the best that the Whites were in charge, and even the abolitionists were not above such thoughts. Only the most radical abolitionists advocated racial equality – often Quakers, who believed that all people were equal in the eyes of God. William Wilberforce certainly did not. After the slaves were free, he expected them to continue to serve Whites as a 'grateful peasantry'.[4]

The racism of conquest

Racial superiority allowed Britain, and later the United States, to explain away slavery as the natural order of things. Perhaps even the God-given order of things. It also underlies imperial conquest.

The lightning rod for imperial racism is Cecil Rhodes, a man whose ego bestrode entire continents. Hailing from Hertfordshire, the same county where I was born, Rhodes made his fortune in the diamond mines of South Africa. He used his wealth and influence to expand the British Empire, with the vast territories of Rhodesia named after him.*

For Rhodes, expanding White rule was 'a duty': 'more territory simply means more of the Anglo-Saxon race, more of the best, the most human, the most honourable race the world possesses.'[5] It is hardly surprising that equality campaigners have objected to statues, buildings and scholarships in his honour.

Imperialists could appeal to science for backup. There was the pseudoscience of Phrenology, which claimed that intellect and character could be read from the shape of a person's head. Darwin's theories of evolution were also ripe for misuse. His work is certainly open to racist interpretations, with *The Descent of Man* discussing 'savage' and 'civilised races', and how the 'distinct races' of man 'may be more appropriately called sub-species'.[6]

Expansion could be justified religiously too. The imperial hymn 'Land of Hope and Glory' was first performed in 1902, a month after Britain's victory in the Boer war. That was a war for control of gold and diamond reserves, and in which Britain invented the concentration camp. And yet Elgar casually frames this conquest as the will of God in the song's chorus: 'Wider and still wider, shall thy bounds be set. God who made thee mighty make thee mightier yet.'

---

* Now Zimbabwe and Zambia. Among the few countries that are still named after their White invaders are Colombia and the Philippines.

This is not unique to Britain, of course. When the conquistadors set foot in South America, their brutal subjugation of the indigenous people was fully sanctioned by the Pope. In a series of decrees, Pope Alexander VI explained how all nations not currently occupied by Christians could rightfully be settled, thereby expanding the faith.[7] This 'doctrine of discovery' justified conquest and oppression, and the misuse of religion was not lost on those who were enslaved. 'The god of the White man inspires him with crime, but our god calls upon us to do good works,' said the Haitian revolutionary and Vodou priest Boukman Dutty in 1791. 'Throw away the symbol of the God of the Whites who has so often caused us to weep.'[8]

Plunder

It is easy enough to argue that slavery and empire were racist projects. What is important for our purposes here is that they feed directly into industrialisation, and thus the climate crisis.

Colonialism captured the productive capacity of overseas lands. For a small country such as Britain, the Empire massively expanded its reach, with all resources flowing home to the centre. Slavery harnessed human labour for the benefit of the home country. These two factors — free land and free labour — acted as a huge subsidy to Western development. They provided the capital for industrialisation and account for a large part of global inequality today.

This can be quite directly traced. When slavery was finally abolished in 1833, the slave owners — rather than the slaves

– were compensated for their loss.* The Treasury paid a huge sum in compensation, equivalent to 5 per cent of the nation's GDP at the time, and the records that were kept provide a remarkable list of who owned slaves and how many. Those records only became publicly available in 2013, and they can be browsed online, alongside further information about the slave owners' other interests.[9]

Some slave owners put their money into stately homes or built museums, churches or key infrastructure. Clifton Suspension Bridge and Bristol Zoo were built by the slave magnate Thomas Daniel. The Earl Talbot was an investor in two estates in Jamaica, where over 500 slaves worked between them. He used his wealth to create the Staffordshire gardens of Alton Towers, now the site of one of the country's leading theme parks.

It gets closer to home than one might expect. My children attended Crawley Green School, and walked down Crawley Green Road to get there. Samuel Crawley was an important Luton resident and the owner of the Stockwood estate, now a park and discovery centre. Listed among Crawley's many interests were two coffee plantations in Grenada that used slave labour.[10]

Five minutes' walk in the other direction is my local pub, one of the 2,700 pubs and restaurants operated by the Greene King brewery company, whose beers are stocked in

---

* This expense was so big that it was only paid off in full in 2015, meaning that I have personally contributed through my taxes to compensating slave owners – and so have generations of Black British citizens.

every cornershop, off-licence and supermarket in the land. The founder, Benjamin Greene, was a slave owner who lobbied parliament on behalf of slavers, and who worked to undermine the reputation of abolitionists.[11]

As well as buildings and businesses, the profits from slavery were invested into Britain's own productive capacity. The records show slave-owners' wealth being ploughed into Britain's railway building boom. Others invested in shipbuilding, mining or manufacturing. Much of the wealth went into the banking sector, which in turn provided the finance for industry.

The Caribbean historian Eric Williams, later the first prime minister of Trinidad and Tobago, was one of the first to detail these connections in his 1944 book *Capitalism and Slavery*. He pointed out that the most iconic invention of the era, James Watt's steam engine, was funded with a loan from a bank financed by the plantations of the West Indies.[12]

Britain takes great pride in the Industrial Revolution – enough to have made it a feature of the opening ceremony of the London Olympic Games in 2012. The story is told with a focus on the ingenuity of the inventors and engineers, and rarely on how it was funded. The reality is that it was the huge input of stolen land, labour and resources from the slave colonies that enabled Britain and Western Europe to industrialise.

First Spain and Portugal, then Britain, France and Germany, Belgium and Italy, and several others, all profited from this plundering of resources and labour. The United States was also built on genocidal land theft and slavery – 'people turned to fuel for the American machine', in the words of the essayist Ta-Nehisi Coates.[13]

The anthropologist Jason Hickel proposes a thought experiment: 'What if the sum of the value produced by African slaves in the New World – worth the equivalent of trillions of dollars today – was subtracted from Western wealth and added to the total wealth of Africa?'[14]

This matters because, with slavery, it is easy to focus on the abuse suffered by the slaves themselves and miss the absence they left behind. 'Slavery happened to Africa as much as it did to those who arrived in the Americas or the Caribbean,' says the British race scholar Kehinde Andrews.[15] The West's gain in stolen people was Africa's loss, a setback that has echoed through the centuries.

What if the gold and silver from South America are added to the bill? The diamonds from South Africa? The looted treasures in Western museums? The cheap cotton from India? The land from the Native Americans and the Aboriginal Australians? For centuries, the global North took what it wanted. Defenders of empire insist that colonialism brought benefits too, but the priorities of empire were clear: the extraction of value from 'inferior' people and lands.

The logic of climate change isn't so very different. The big emitters extract fossil fuels, often in 'sacrifice zones' in distant countries, and burn them to drive economic growth back home. Then they dump their pollution into a global atmosphere, and shift the consequences on others in distant parts of the world.

As with slavery and colonialism, the perpetrators are mostly White, and those plundered are people of colour.

Independence without freedom

Independence came to Africa in stages, mainly between 1955 and 1975. Even as country after country was signed over to local rule, campaigners for independence could see the threat of ongoing Western dominance. The All-African People's Conference, held in 1961, offered a definition of 'neocolonialism' as 'the survival of the colonial system in spite of the formal recognition of political independence'. Right from the start, African leaders had identified 'an indirect and subtle form of domination by political, economic, social, military or technical means'.[16]

Kwame Nkrumah, the first president of Ghana, expanded on this idea in his book *Neo-Colonialism: The Last Stage of Imperialism*. Among the 'mechanisms of neo-colonialism' that he describes are high interest rates, control of world markets, *coups d'état* against African leaders, and putting conditions on financial aid in order to manipulate domestic policy.[17] On publication in 1965, the United States proved the point by withholding aid, and just four months later Nkrumah was deposed in a CIA-assisted coup.[18] The new military leadership conveniently pivoted away from socialist alliances and turned towards the West, and Nkrumah saw out the rest of his life in exile.

Walter Rodney was one of the first to raise awareness of these issues and connect them to the broader story of slavery and empire. Born in Guyana in South America, he travelled extensively in the Caribbean and in Africa and became known as a radical pan-African scholar and activist. While working as a university professor in Tanzania in 1972, he published the landmark book *How Europe Underdeveloped Africa*.

'Foreign ownership is still present, although the armies and flags of foreign powers have been removed,' he observed. 'So long as foreigners own land, mines, factories, banks, insurance companies, means of transportation, newspapers, power stations, then for so long will the wealth of Africa flow outwards.'[19] The colonies had been given political freedom, but not economic freedom.

Western interests still controlled the assets and infrastructure, the rights to natural resources and the means of production. The old powers controlled the terms of trade, meaning that 'the whole import-export relationship between Africa and its trading partners is one of unequal exchange and of exploitation'.

Walter Rodney was killed by political opponents in 1980, using a bomb hidden in a walkie-talkie. Responsibility for his assassination has never been established.

Underdevelopment

It wasn't enough to exploit and extract from the colonies. There have always been policies to restrain development too. Britain used its colonies to produce raw materials, and these were then shipped to Britain for manufacturing, with the finished goods often sold back to the colonies again. This captured the value at home in the British economy. It was one of the drivers of the movement for Indian independence: India was forbidden to spin its own cloth, and Gandhi advocated the simple act of spinning thread at home as an act of civil disobedience.

Sometimes these kinds of prohibitions could be deadly. During the Bengal famine of 1943, British administrators insisted that food exports to Britain continue even as the crisis took hold. There was enough food in the region to feed everyone, but millions of people nevertheless starved. Amartya Sen lived through the famine as a child, and later studied the crisis. Starvation, he concluded, 'is a function of entitlements – and not of food availability'.[20]

The micro-managing of food and resources did not end with the collapse of the colonial era and independence. Even programmes that were supposed to help were compromised in their objectives. Zambian economist Dambisa Moyo has described how development aid comes with all kinds of strings attached that benefit the donor countries and lock poorer countries into dependence.[21]

In the 1990s and early 2000s economists such as Joseph Stiglitz and Ha-Joon Chang blew the whistle on how the International Monetary Fund and the World Bank wrote international rules to favour the richest. For years poorer countries were advised – as a condition of development aid – to produce for export and not attempt to industrialise. They were instructed to open their markets to foreign competition and denationalise prize assets. They were forbidden from subsidising industries or farmers, while the US and the EU ran generous subsidy schemes for their own producers and crowded developing world producers out of global markets.

All of this kept the profits flowing back to the West. As Chang summarised it in his book *Kicking Away the Ladder*, 'the developed countries did not get where they are now through the policies and the institutions that they recommend to developing countries today'.[22]

Many Western commentators continue to use a one-word riposte to these sorts of arguments: corruption. And while it is true that many African leaders (including Kwame Nkrumah), have a troubled legacy, many of Africa's worst dictators were installed or supported by Western forces. Nnimmo Bassey, the Nigerian environmentalist and poet, points out a double standard. African countries are often accused of corruption, while 'scant attention' is paid to corporate tax dodging, with the full cooperation of the global accountancy firms, which robs African governments of billions of dollars every year.[23] By facilitating capital flight out of Africa, corruption is itself a tool of neo-colonialism, allowing Western interests to bypass the processes of democracy and public scrutiny.

The slaves may be free, the old colonies independent. But the power imbalance remains, in the form of the ongoing structural racism of international relations.

Ecological debt

Slavery and colonialism funded industrialisation, and thus lie at the heart of climate change. They are an unpaid debt, and climate change can be added to that ledger. 'If you take more than your fair share of a finite natural resource you run up an ecological debt,' suggests the economist Andrew Simms in his book on the topic.[24] Some countries run a huge surplus of greenhouse gases, relying on others to run a deficit that mops up their pollution. Yet the damage will not fall on the polluters, making them climate free-riders.

Ecological debt flips the conventional debt relationship on its head. Poorer developing countries are usually the ones seen as debtors, owing billions to the banks and governments of the rich world. From a carbon point of view, the richer nations are in debt to the poor who live well below their means in terms of carbon footprint. Will that debt ever be paid?

In his encyclical *Laudato Si'*, Pope Francis spells out the moral implication of this debt: 'Developing countries, where the most important reserves of the biosphere are found, continue to fuel the development of richer countries at the cost of their own present and future ... The developed countries ought to help pay this debt by significantly limiting their consumption of non-renewable energy and by assisting poorer countries to support policies and programmes of sustainable development.'[25]

Whites in charge

'Thinking about the British Empire,' asks the polling agency YouGov, 'would you say it is more something to be proud of or more something to be ashamed of?' It's 2014 and the Commonwealth Games are coming up – an event where

Britain's former colonies compete sportingly as friends. Britain is hosting the event in Glasgow, and there's a positive buzz about the occasion. A sense of *bonhomie* prevails, and nobody will mention the darker side of empire – the slavery and mass displacement, the wars of aggression, the famines and genocide. Yes, say 59 per cent of British respondents. The Empire is something to be proud of.

'Would you like Britain to still have an empire?' the survey goes on. Yes, say 34 per cent.[26]

Boris Johnson, later to become prime minister, took a similarly positive line when writing about Africa. 'The problem is not that we were once in charge, but that we are not in charge any more,' he wrote in the *Spectator* in 2002. 'The best fate for Africa would be if the old colonial powers, or their citizens, scrambled once again in her direction.'[27]

The idea that White people should be in charge doesn't seem to have gone anywhere.

Injustice upon injustice

Climate change arises out of a historical context, and so it reflects the injustices of its time. It is a product of injustice, and it perpetuates the injustices that lie behind it. As the academic activist Janine Francois puts it simply: 'climate change is the outcome of White Western colonialism'.[28]

Again, climate change cannot 'be' racist with any kind of intent. Only people can be racist in the most obvious interpretation of the word. But the climate crisis arises from racial injustice and the plundering of the global South, and it is in itself a form of exploitation of the global South.

The climate crisis is not generally described in these terms, but it is not news to race activists. 'The impact of climate change on black and brown-skinned people comes on the back of 500 years of exploitation of their bodies anyway,' the theologian Anthony Reddie told me. 'It's a compound disaster, adding one injustice to another ... The people who suffered 500 years ago are the same ones suffering now.'[29]

Climate violence

I n May 2020, George Floyd was killed in the street. A White police officer knelt on his neck for almost nine minutes, well past the point when he had stopped saying 'I can't breathe'. Bystanders filmed the whole thing, and I cried when I saw the footage. I cried for George. I cried at the fragility of life. I cried at the powerlessness of the bystanders, pleading 'check his pulse!'

Millions responded in outrage, as protestors ignored curfews and took their anger to the streets. Former president Donald Trump – a Venn diagram of affluent detachment, White privilege and toxic masculinity – focused on the violence and said little about the reasons for it. He boasted about the 'vicious dogs' awaiting anyone who crossed the White House perimeter. He tweeted all-caps invocations such as 'LAW & ORDER' – a concern that was notably absent when his own followers stormed the Capitol Building a matter of months later.

Black Lives Matter

Police brutality is currently the most high-profile aspect of racial injustice. Young Black men in America are twice as likely to be killed by the police as their White counterparts.[1] To take the 2015 figures, for which there is good data, a total of 1,134 people were killed by the police in the United States. Over half of them were from ethnic minorities. And yet, not a single police officer was convicted of murder in 2015.[2] Not even Timothy Loehmann, who shot and killed twelve-year-old Tamir Rice in a public park in Cleveland. Tamir was playing with a toy gun. Loehmann opened fire within two seconds of arriving on the scene.[3]

Young Black men are also more likely to be arrested, charged and imprisoned. 12 per cent of the US population is Black, as is a third of its prison population.[4]

Black Lives Matter was founded in 2013 to highlight these injustices, after the shooting of Trayvon Martin. The movement has grown, but, despite the steps forward in awareness, the problem remains. History keeps repeating itself, and the resurfacing of tensions in 2020 should hardly have come as a surprise. 'Oppressed people cannot remain oppressed forever,' as Martin Luther King, Jr. warned in 1963.[5]

The climate connection

In September 2016, activists managed to breach the security of London City Airport and get onto the runway. There they erected a tripod and locked themselves onto and around it. Flights were disrupted for around six hours and 131 planes were rerouted before police could dismantle the protest. Nine arrests were made.

The action was carried out by Black Lives Matter UK (BLM UK), and the banners they laid out on the ground read: 'The climate crisis is a racist crisis.' The action was carried out to 'highlight the UK's environmental impact on the lives of Black people locally and globally', BLM UK said in a statement. 'Black people are the first to die, not the first to fly, in this racist climate crisis.'

As well as making the connection between climate change and the global inequality of its effects, the protesters' choice of City Airport is also significant because it is in the London borough of Newham. London is already the most ethnically diverse city in Britain, and Newham has the smallest percentage of White residents of any local authority in the country, at 29 per cent.[6] It is an archetypal 'sacrifice zone' – a poorer district with a disproportionate number of Black and Asian residents who put up with more than their fair share of noise and pollution. City Airport, meanwhile, serves the elite business travellers of London's financial centre. It's a totemic example of inequality, and its plans to expand further into Newham would later make the airport a target for Extinction Rebellion.

It was perhaps the first time that climate and race were connected in the British press, though it was widely misunderstood. 'Have you been hijacked?' the BBC asked a BLM UK spokesperson.[7] The *Daily Mail* complained that 'all of those involved were White and all from privileged backgrounds', even though this was a deliberate decision.[8] Even some antiracism campaigners were divided on the protest, wondering if it was a distraction from the real issues. What did flying have to do with Black Lives Matter?

Alexandra Wanjiku Kelbert, one of the protest organisers, explained BLM UK's actions: 'When we say Black lives matter, we mean *all* Black lives, and that includes the lives of those who live in proximity to airports, to power plants, to the busiest of roads, and whose children grow up with asthma and skin conditions exacerbated by air pollution.'[9]

I can't breathe

Reading Wanjiku Kelbert's words about London children growing up with air pollution, one particular child comes to mind: Ella Kissi-Debrah. After suffering from respiratory problems for several years, she died in 2013 after a particularly severe asthma attack. She was nine years old.

Her mother, Rosamund Kissi-Debrah, knew that air pollution in their area of London was a factor in her condition and therefore in her death. But, as is usually the case, the official cause of death was recorded as asthma. It was only after a long legal case that an inquest ruled in 2020: 'Ella died of asthma, contributed to by exposure to excessive air pollution.' It was the first time that a coroner in the UK had named air pollution as a cause of death.[10]

London's Black residents face greater exposure to air pollution, and some of the city's most polluted districts have large Black populations.[11] There is a racial dimension to air pollution in London, another example of environmental injustice, and an echo of the Black Lives Matter rallying cry 'I can't breathe'.

Black Lives Matter has mainly been associated with police brutality and mass incarceration, with violence against Black people. But in counting the cost of climate change or air pollution, isn't environmental harm also a form of violence?

Structural violence

Racism can be understood as prejudiced actions and opinions, as we saw in the Introduction. It can also be understood as structural, embedded in cultural and social patterns. Violence is similar. The most obvious form is direct or inter-personal violence, when one person's actions are seen to harm somebody else. But violence has deeper dimensions.

The idea of structural violence was first developed by Johan Galtung in the 1960s. Galtung was an early practitioner of what is now called Peace Studies, a social studies discipline that deliberately distanced peacebuilding and conflict resolution from the study of conflict itself. He argued that violence can be understood at three levels.

- At the bottom is *cultural violence* – long-standing attitudes such as White supremacy or male superiority, for example.
- This cultural violence legitimises *structural violence*, which emerges as patterns of disadvantage such as racial or gender inequality.
- The third level is the acts of *direct violence* that reflect the inequality: police shootings, or acts of violence against women.

Understood in this wider perspective, violence flows upwards from deep roots. Violent acts flow from inequalities which in turn flow from culture.

Only the top strata requires intent. Direct violence is a deliberate act, whereas structural violence results from 'numerous acts of omission'.[12] Structural violence is better understood as a process than an event. The suffering that it causes can be many times greater than direct violence, but it goes unnoticed because it is de-personified and diffused across many people and many different acts. It is the grinding inequality that holds minorities back, year after year.

Environmental inequalities are an example of structural violence. They too flow from deep cultural ideas about who is entitled to clean air and water, and who is less 'deserving'. Who must be kept safe and who is, to quote a Robert D. Bullard book title, the 'wrong complexion for protection'?[13]

Slow violence

Archona and Priambandhu were farmers in Kaya Benia, a village in Bangladesh. In previous years they had been able to produce two tonnes of rice from their eleven acres of land. After repeated cyclones and floods, their land has shrunk to two acres and what remains is polluted with salt. It is underwater for four months of the year.

'We don't know the future, but we can assume that we will lose it all,' says Archona. 'We are losing our home. We have lost our livelihood and we are fighting to have enough food and water for each day. If we just had the land beneath our feet, then we could adapt to climate change.'[14]

Archona and Priambandhu have suffered an act of violence. Their home and their livelihood has been destroyed. Their land has been taken from them. They have contributed almost nothing to the crisis – as Constance Okollet said in Chapter 1, this is something that has been done to them.

The cause and the effect are so far apart from each other that it might not be recognised as violence. There was no malicious intent, and yet their experience is all too common. As greenhouse gases pollute the atmosphere from the world's most developed countries, the waters rise or the rains fail in faraway places. Heatwaves claim the weakest. Crops are lost. Places and the memories they hold are erased. Cultural heritage is eroded. The individual events – the storms and cyclones – are sometimes described as 'violent'. Why not the wider issue?

If the cause and the effect could be connected, perhaps it would be more obvious that expanding an airport, opening a new coal mine or pulling out of an international treaty are acts of violence. They are acts of violence perpetrated against nature and biodiversity, and against people of colour.

One reason that climate change is not seen as violence is that it happens so gradually. This is a problem identified by Rob Dixon, a professor at Princeton's High Meadows Environmental Institute. He describes how environmental harm progresses as 'slow violence': 'a violence that occurs gradually and out of sight, a violence of delayed destruction that is dispersed across time and space, an attritional violence that is typically not viewed as violence at all'.[15]

Climate violence

Climate change is nobody's fault. Nobody intended it. It has not been designed. It has been 'created by generations of decisions from privileged people who seek to make themselves safe and comfortable, who contribute disproportionately to the problem of climate change while tending to avoid its worst effects'.[16]

That's Kevin J. O'Brien, who argues that climate change is a problem of structural violence in his striking book *The Violence of Climate Change*. 'It has no single architect and no direct cause, but it is nevertheless violence – a selfish expression of power that harms others.'

The book discusses structural violence and presents historical case studies in non-violent resistance as possible responses to the climate crisis. It isn't specifically about race, but in adding the conclusions from earlier chapters to his insights, I reach an uncomfortable conclusion:

Climate change is racial violence.

There is a through line from George Floyd in Minneapolis to Archona and Priambandhu in Bangladesh. They have all suffered from acts of violence that spring from underlying patterns of inequality, where some people's lives have greater value than others'. The convenience of White consumers, the right to drive or fly or eat beef, takes precedence over the rights of Black and Brown people around the world.

As demonstrators took to the streets of Minneapolis in May 2020, climate activists from the local branch of 350.org served food and provided first aid to protestors. Sam Grant, executive director and environmental justice campaigner, made the connection very clearly: 'Police violence is an aspect of a broader pattern of structural violence, which the climate crisis is a manifestation of.'[17]

It is all part of the same struggle, the defiant cry that Black Lives Matter.

The maangamizi

The British media may have been wrong-footed by the actions of Black Lives Matter UK, and their assertion that climate change is racist. African activists would have been less surprised.

Maangamizi is a Swahili word that means havoc or annihilation. It has become a shorthand term for an 'Afrikan holocaust' that stretches from slavery, through colonialism and into current oppression and the threat of climate change. It is used by pan-African activists and academics, including a group who run a petition called 'Stop the Maangamizi: We charge genocide/ecocide'.

'We have our own understanding of the problem of climate change, within the context of Pan-Afrikan Internationalism,' write Kofi Mawuli Klu and Esther Stanford-Xosei from the Pan-Afrikan Reparations Coalition in Europe (PARCOE). The group 'sees climate change as one of the results of the criminal imposition – by the ruling classes of Europe – of a rapacious system expropriating the resources of the globe, not only at the expense of the majority of Humanity, but also to the detriment of our Mother Earth'.[18]

The term genocide is not an exaggeration. The first genocide of the 20th century was in German-controlled West Africa, a campaign called the *Vernichtung* that drove out the Herero and Nama tribespeople. *The Times of Israel* described it as a 'template for the Holocaust'.[19] Similar atrocities occurred in the Congo under Belgium, Libya under Italian rule, and the French colonies in Algeria. Other crimes may not fit the specific definition of genocide, but what is the right word for systematically obliterating an entire culture, as British imperialist forces did in the sacking of Benin?*

While colonialism may have formally ended, pan-Africans argue that justice is yet to be done and the damage is ongoing. As the rapper Akala puts it, 'They changed that much? Are you so sure? The world's darker people still the most poor?'[20]

This history of genocide and extraction of value from Africa is now being compounded by the climate crisis. It has taken different forms over the centuries, but the same pattern of cultural violence underlies slavery, colonisation, unfair trade rules and the climate crisis. First it was the people and their labour. Then

---

* In 1897 British forces destroyed the ancient royal city of Benin in what is now Nigeria, burned it to the ground and built a golf course on the site of the king's house. The tens of thousands of African casualties were never counted. Extensive collections of the looted treasure can still be found in the British Museum and elsewhere.

it was the land and the resources. Now it is the atmosphere. The nature of the plunder has changed, but the logic remains the same: White people are entitled to take what they need from Black people.

'I'm going to be greedy for the United States,' promised Donald Trump on the campaign trail. 'I'm going to take and take and take. We're going to take, take, take, take.'[21]

7

Climate privilege

> 'The point about coal is that it has produced enormous
> improvement in human living standards — and not just
> coal, same with oil, same with gas, same with all three fossil
> fuels. The improvement that they have done to human life
> is spectacular, but not just to human life, to the planet as
> well. And people somehow think that fossil fuels are evil.'[1]

This is Matt Ridley, a science writer, former banker, peer of the
realm and one of Britain's most prominent climate sceptics. He
is part of the landed gentry and the owner of the Blagdon Hall
estate in Northumberland.

The estate is home to two coal mines.

Ridley acknowledges the conflict of interest, and says his
views on climate change would be no different if his family
did not profit from coal. Maybe so. Perhaps there is a parallel
dimension where Matt Ridley does not have coal mines on his
family land, and where he is still a climate sceptic. Until that
dimension is found, there is no way to test his claim.

In the last chapter I described the deep roots of the climate
crisis. It emerges from an already divided and unequal world,

and environmental injustice reflects all the intersecting injustices of the past. In this chapter I want to look at some of the ways that these inequalities are perpetuated, and how privilege acts to protect the status quo.

Profiting from denial

Climate change has been understood for a long time. The Swedish scientist Svante Arrhenius explained how CO_2 emissions from industry were changing the temperature right back in 1896.[2] The metaphor of a greenhouse effect had been used 70 years earlier by the French physicist Jean-Baptiste Joseph Fourier. And 50 years before him, the less well-known but magnificently named Georges-Louis Leclerc de Buffon had described how the Earth's atmosphere could be affected by human behaviour.[3] There's really little reason for climate science to still be controversial.

It became more controversial as the projections became observable – and, more importantly, as the calls to address it began to grow. Scientists at the Exxon oil company made a study of climate change in the early 1980s. Their briefing paper notes that 'mitigation of the "greenhouse effect" would require major reductions in fossil fuel combustion'.[4] The briefing is available online today, but at the time it came with a note to say it should not be distributed externally. Similar research from Shell a few years later was also kept confidential.

The oil companies knew about climate change and knew that it directly affected their business. A deliberate choice was made to ignore the science rather than compromise profits. For some, it went further than ignoring it. Climate science was actively suppressed. Funding poured into lobby groups and sympathetic think tanks, spreading alternative 'scientific' explanations. A movement emerged, with its own websites and conferences and superstars. It's a story well-documented in books such as Naomi Oreskes and Erik Conway's *Merchants of Doubt* or George Monbiot's *Heat*.

The movement eroded trust in climate science, which in turn played a role in the collapse of the Copenhagen climate talks in 2009. It felt for a while as if the sceptics had won, and every mention of climate change was a battle. Even my relatively insignificant environmental website, The Earthbound Report, came under sustained attack. A little digging into the trolling comments below every climate-related post revealed them to be deliberately coordinated by a small network. The abuse I experienced was trivial compared to the insults, character assassinations and even death threats received by leading climate scientists and campaigners.

We will never know how many were silenced, but we do know who gains from the confusion and the delay: the fossil fuel industry, the polluter elite who benefit from it, and the governments that derive their power from it.

Networks of influence

Let's come back to Matt Ridley for a moment. It's nothing personal; he's just a useful example.

In 2012, on his father's death, Ridley inherited the title of 5th Viscount Ridley and Baron Wensleydale. The following year he was appointed as a hereditary peer in the House of Lords. Unelected by British voters, he has a seat for life in the upper house, able to vote for or against every climate change or energy-related bill that passes before him. Within months he had breached the code of conduct by speaking in favour of fracking while failing to mention that he had investments in the sector.[5]

Ridley already had influence. His brother-in-law is Owen Paterson, who served as environment minister under David Cameron's Conservative government, despite – or perhaps because of – his climate-sceptic views. His uncle was a Conservative MP. He comes from the same Eton and Oxford stock as many Conservative politicians.

And he already had a platform. As well as his own books and website, he has been a science and environment columnist for *The Times* and the *Wall Street Journal*. Both of those were part of the Rupert Murdoch media empire at the time – an empire that includes *Fox News* in the US, and the Australian newspapers that supported Scott Morrison and his climate-sceptic policies.

The White men who run the world have money, political influence and a media platform. They are able to deploy all of these to steward their own interests, and that may not even be a conscious decision. Remember – a structural injustice does not need intent. Self-serving climate arguments don't have to involve corporate plots or dark money, though sometimes they do. They are just as much to do with old-boys' networks, peer pressure and group-think.

The system is self-reinforcing. A politician will get their news from their preferred outlet, which has likely become their preferred news outlet because it reflects their worldview. They will hear opinions and new ideas from the organisations and associations that they already take an interest in. If they have a question or seek more information, it is likely to be raised with friends and colleagues within their own circles.

Since White Anglo-Saxon men are among the most privileged people in human history, concerns about justice don't surface very often. These are capitalism's winners, climate winners, the beneficiaries of race and gender inequality. 'Those with privilege,' writes Jennie Stephens in her book *Diversifying Power*, 'are generally less aware of the structural oppression that stratifies society than those without such privilege, which is why antiracist, feminist leadership is so critical.'[6]

I'm alright, Jack

Apologies to his lordship, but here's Matt Ridley again, this time in the sarcastically titled book *Climate Change: The Facts*.[7] Ridley does not deny that climate change is happening; rather, he argues that it will be positive: 'the harm is currently smaller than the good [climate change] is doing, through longer growing seasons, milder winters, slightly higher rainfall, and faster growth rates of crops and forests because of CO_2 fertilisation.

And that net good stands in stark contrast to the net harm caused by climate change policy.'

When someone argues that climate change is positive, the immediate question is 'for whom?'

For the world's most vulnerable, climate change is already devastating. What's a longer growing season worth if your land has been flooded with seawater? Or higher rainfall if it washes away your crops and topsoil? And 'milder winters'? Imagine the reaction that comment would get in Turbat in Pakistan. For Black and minority ethnic people, for indigenous communities, the idea of climate change as positive is laughable. But they don't have the money, political influence or platform.

For the polluter elite, however, Ridley isn't wrong. At least in the short term, it is action to prevent climate change that presents a bigger risk. Governments might ban coal power, tax pollution or support the renewable energy that will erode their profits.

Even that apparent immunity won't last forever. The climate crisis will affect everyone eventually, through mounting costs and increasing instability. Ultimately the whole planet will become inhospitable if runaway climate change cannot be averted.

The political turning point may be occurring at the moment, following the escalation in urgency in recent years, and Joe Biden's reset of American priorities. The sceptics' own children may change their minds, as Rupert Murdoch's youngest son James has apparently been trying to do.[8] But it certainly has been true, for the last 30 or 40 years, that action to stop climate change is against the immediate interests of the polluter elite.

The intersectionality of denial

There are some big funders and influential people behind climate denial, but it also has a grassroots. Millions of people are united in their opposition to carbon targets and policies to prevent climate change. Perhaps unsurprisingly, given what we have seen about overlapping layers of disadvantage, there are overlapping layers of privilege too. People who fear that their privileged position is being undermined on one axis of inequality may be more likely to oppose action on other inequalities.

Salil Benegal, an American social scientist, has studied attitudes towards race and climate change. He found that 'high levels of racial resentment are strongly correlated with reduced agreement with the scientific consensus on climate change'.[9] That's not to say that all those who disagree with climate science are racists, but there is a correlation: a high score on tests of racial prejudice and racial resentment were a strong indicator that people would also reject climate science.

Benegal observed that this tendency increased after the election of Barack Obama. In the early years of the Obama presidency, levels of agreement with climate science stayed the same among Black voters. Among White Americans, it fell by 18 per cent. If somebody felt that their identity or lifestyle was challenged by a Black president, they were likely to feel that action on climate change was a threat to their identity or lifestyle too.

Surveys of attitudes to climate change in America show higher levels of concern among people of colour. 69 per cent of Latinos are 'alarmed' or 'concerned' about the climate, 57 per cent of Black Americans and 49 per cent of White Americans. White people are twice as likely to be doubtful or dismissive.[10]

That which must not be named

A couple of years ago I was working in an open-plan office, and a colleague was talking about his recent holiday. He had flown to the States and hired a sports car for a road trip. We were just getting to an anecdote about a Texan barbecue when he remembered I was in the room. (I hadn't said anything. Apparently I have this effect on people.) The combined weight of aviation + sports car + beef must have tipped the balance of his moral scales.

He looked at me and shrugged. 'I know, I probably should have hired a Prius instead of the Dodge.'

Everyone laughed, and the passing mention of climate responsibility was brushed aside.

I'm sure you will have experienced something similar – an uncomfortable pause, an awkward laugh, a hasty change of subject. It's very rare for anyone to actually press into that moment of recognition – 'Yes, why didn't you hire the Prius?' Or better yet, 'If you wanted a road trip, why didn't you drive to the South of France or somewhere you didn't have to fly to first?'

It's not like it doesn't come up. There are heatwaves, wildfires in the news, torrential downpours, unseasonal blossom on the trees. And still, it so rarely gets discussed. The sociologist Eviatar Zerubavel calls this 'disattention': 'when we deliberately fail to notice something and cannot even explain that silence'.[11]

Another common response is to explain away culpability. Cost is a common one, when people say that they can't afford ethical fashion or vegan food. Claiming confusion is another: 'I just don't know where to start.' Blaming China remains enduringly popular, or saying that our own actions won't make any difference. Kari Marie Norgaard, a sociologist who studies conversations around climate change, describes these as 'tools of innocence'. When climate change comes up, there's always a plug-and-play reason why it can't have anything to do with me.

Painful though it may be to admit, inequalities are perpetuated through such small things as conversations at barbecues and at the school gates. As Norgaard warns: 'The construction of denial and innocence work to silence the needs and voices of women and people of colour in the Global South, and thus reproduce global inequality along the lines of gender, race and class.'[12]

It would be easier to peg climate denial as a problem for fossil fuel lobbyists and right-wing think tanks. But the most common form of denial is silence. It's the way a married couple might never get round to discussing their credit card debt, or how a group might never challenge a friend's obviously unhealthy drinking habit. It hovers there unacknowledged because it's too stressful to think about.

This is a very human reaction. Humans deny 'the things we don't want to admit exist', as Haydn Washington and John Cook say in their book *Climate Change Denial*.[13] And where climate silence meets White privilege, that's a very quiet place indeed.

Climate privilege

'Ignorance of how we are shaped racially is the first sign of privilege,' says the antiracism educator Tim Wise. 'It is a privilege to ignore the consequences of race in America.'[14] The race commentator Reni Eddo-Lodge summarises White privilege as 'an absence of the negative consequences of racism'.[15]

I think a very direct parallel could be drawn: ignoring the consequences of climate change is a form of privilege. It is a luxury to not have to worry about it, to be free of its negative consequences. Let's call it climate privilege.

Climate privilege is when you can think about the climate emergency as an environmental issue. As you're not a polar bear, it's not something that keeps you awake at night. If you have thought of climate change as something that will affect the future, that's a sign of climate privilege: for many it is right here and right now.

If you've been able to cut your carbon footprint and feel like you've done your bit, there's an element of privilege to that too. Those who are most vulnerable have footprints so small that there's nothing to cut, and they experience climate change as something that is done to them, not something that we're all bound up in collectively.

If you have never experienced climate change as harm, as loss, as injustice or as violence, you are privileged.

There is a big overlap between climate privilege and White privilege.

I appreciate that this is difficult territory. I am both of those things myself, and here again, let me stress the point I made in the Introduction: privilege is not okay, but it is not my fault. Each of us are born into different patterns of advantage and disadvantage. I cannot be blamed for being privileged, but I can be held responsible for what I do with it.

That's a bit of a balancing act, recognising responsibility without accepting blame. The songwriter Courtney Ariel describes it this way, in an article advising her White friends on supporting antiracism:

'Privilege means that you owe a debt. You were born with it. You didn't ask for it. And you didn't pay for it either. No one is blaming you for having it. You are lovely, human and amazing. Being a citizen of a society requires work from everyone within that society. It is up to you whether you choose to acknowledge the work that is yours to do. It is up to you whether you choose to pay this debt and how you choose to do so.'[16]

The empathy gap

When the virus first arrived in the country, Bintu Sannoh was not worried. 'Then, in early August, the situation changed. The government banned all movements in and out of Kenema and Kailahun districts. Everything came to a standstill. We were trapped.'

'In less than two weeks, seventeen people died from five households, with nine more admitted to hospital. Next we saw a group of fearfully dressed men from the hospital. They entered our home and brought out the mattresses and bedding and set them all on fire, spraying inside all the bedrooms and parlour. I watched with tears in my eyes as they did the same thing in every house where someone had died or contracted the virus. That sight was terrifying.'[1]

Many more of us know what a medical emergency lockdown looks like today, but not like this one. Bintu, thirteen at the time, is describing the Ebola outbreak in Sierra Leone in 2014.

It is hard to imagine a more nightmarish disease than Ebola, with a 50 per cent survival rate and a long recovery process for those that do pull through. It first surfaced in 1976, and there have been over twenty outbreaks since, all of them in Sub-Saharan Africa. A vaccine for Ebola was finally deployed for the first time during an outbreak in 2019.[2]

It took over 40 years for an Ebola vaccine to become available commercially, yet here's the mystery: the first patent for an Ebola vaccine was granted in 2003. The company that acquired the patent did nothing with the research. It sat there unused for a decade. What happened to make them hurry it along?

In September 2014, the first Ebola case on US soil was diagnosed in Texas.[3]

Just two weeks later the company's stock price soared when it announced the start of early vaccine trials.[4]

The value of suffering

Thousands of Black African deaths, widespread trauma and the collapse of national economies over Ebola epidemics were apparently not enough to motivate the patent holders to develop the vaccine they already had. It took just one Ebola case on US soil to spur them into action.

On one level, this is just economics. Because people in the Congo or Sierra Leone are poor, there is little incentive to develop solutions to their problems. Their suffering literally has no value to the pharmaceuticals industry. But Ebola in America – even the fear of an outbreak – sends a powerful market signal.

As before, no deliberate racist attitudes are implied or necessary. As far as we know, no board meeting discussed it and decided to let Black people die of Ebola. The pharmaceuticals industry goes where the money is, and the money is in first world problems.

The pharmaceuticals industry is therefore structurally racist. The logic of the global economy is structurally racist. Because capital resides disproportionately with White people, capitalism itself is structurally racist.

This is a pretty deep rabbit hole.

But let's stick with suffering for a moment, because suffering is at the heart of the climate change debate. John Holdren is a Harvard energy expert and was science advisor to Barack Obama. At the launch of the fourth Intergovernmental Panel on Climate Change (IPCC) report, he said this:

> 'We basically have three choices: mitigation, adaptation and suffering. We're going to do some of each. The question is what the mix is going to be. The more mitigation we do, the less adaptation will be required and the less suffering there will be.'[5]

It's a stark assessment. Climate suffering is rarely acknowledged in political debate, but it will be widespread. It will include losses from drought and famine – people watching their farm dry out and crops fail, their animals sicken and die. It will include hunger, starvation and stunting, and the pain of watching loved ones experience these things. There will be losses from floods, the inundation of homes and gardens, the destruction of cherished objects and all that has been worked for. There will be losses from changed geography: familiar views, landscapes and weather patterns disrupted or obliterated.

Psychological damage will mount. Depression, suicide. There will be fear, uncertainty, confusion.

Cultures and traditions will be lost, with the identity and belonging that they provide. Islamic Relief has warned that 'in a business-as-usual scenario, temperatures in Mecca will rise to a level that the human body cannot cope with'.[6] Imagine the cultural loss that Muslims will face as one of the pillars of Islam becomes a deadly hazard.

Animal suffering should be considered too, and is already with us. It is present in my own back garden at the smallest scale, when butterflies emerge early in an unusually warm winter, only to be killed by a late spring frost. And it is present at the biggest scale elsewhere, such as when elephants starved to death in drought-stricken national parks in Zimbabwe in 2019.

But when John Holdren said 'we're going to do some of each', who does he mean by 'we'? Some are going to suffer a whole lot more than others. There will be more Black suffering than White suffering.

Black suffering

In the research for this book, the most odious text I came across was a book called *The Negroes in Negroland*, by Hinton Rowan Helper. Written in 1868, it describes the supposed 'barbarity' of life in Africa as a justification for slavery. Among the litany of myths in the book is the idea that Black women feel no pain in childbirth and that Black people do not grieve. 'Their grief, if they grieve at all, is but for a moment. Sorrow comes over them and vanishes like the lightning's flash.'[7]

Thank goodness nobody thinks like that anymore. Imagine how it would affect medicine, police restraint procedures, prison sentencing or border policy if people believed that Black people feel less pain.

Except that if a White person turns up at an emergency room in the United States with a broken arm, they will be given pain relief 74 per cent of the time. For Black patients that figure is 57 per cent. Doctors are less likely to prescribe pain medication to Black patients, and prescribe lower doses when they do.[8]

A survey in 2016 presented people with a series of myths about the differences between Black and White bodies – that Black skin was thicker, for example, or that White people had more sensitive nerve endings. Almost three quarters of the general public and around half of medical students believed at least one of the myths. The study concluded that 'people assume a priori that Blacks feel less pain than do Whites'.[9]

Think about how this bias might play out on a global scale. When White people see the news from Pakistan and its record heat levels. When famine hits Ethiopia *again*. Or when a board meeting considers whether or not to invest in that Ebola vaccine they have at the back of the cupboard.

Are White people subconsciously recalibrating the pain levels as they watch the news? Am I, as a White news viewer, doing that?

The empathy gap

In another study, participants had sensors attached to their skin so that researchers could monitor their response to seeing others in pain. Humans can respond physically to another's pain. We flinch. Our palms go sweaty. The researchers showed a series of White participants a video of a syringe needle piercing skin. Three different actors were used – one Caucasian, one Asian and one Black African. Physical responses went in that order, with significantly higher responses to a White person receiving the jab than a Black person, and the Asian person in between.[10]

This is called the 'racial empathy gap', and it has been observed in various contexts. Some suggest it is a factor in harsher prison sentencing, and that it affects the care that Black and minority ethnic patients received during the coronavirus outbreak. Cultural commentators note that romantic comedies with Black leads are less likely to engage White viewers. It turns up in sports, where NFL coaches might be quicker to return an injured Black player to the field.[11]

If this can be observed in legal justice, access to services and policing, it's going to have implications for environmental justice too. This is a major problem for climate change. Earlier chapters have described how it is people of colour who will be hit first and hardest by climate breakdown. The racial empathy gap suggests that this suffering may be discounted by those responsible for it. The problem would be compounded. It would be even harder to build the political will to repair the injustice.

Unnatural disaster

'It's a coastal city,' Daviz Simango reported to the Resilient Cities Congress in 2016. 'As you can imagine, a coastal city is vulnerable to climate change.'[12] The late mayor of Beira, Mozambique, went on to present details of the city's Master Plan 2035, a scheme that would improve flood resilience and protect port infrastructure. Developed with partners in the Netherlands, the Master Plan was a climate adaptation strategy that inspired several other developing world cities.

It came too late. Three years later, tropical cyclone Idai made landfall near the regional capital. Beira was hit by torrential rain and windspeeds of over a hundred miles an hour. The city was flattened. 90 per cent of buildings were lost – the port, schools, hospitals. The electricity and water systems went down.

'The city is destroyed,' said Mayor Simango afterwards. 'We have to start from scratch and we have to prepare for it. Cities have risen from the ashes after world wars in many countries, and Beira too has to rise from the ashes, because it really is destroyed.'[13]

Cyclone Idai was the second deadliest storm ever recorded in the Southern Hemisphere, and it took the number one spot as the most expensive. A thousand people died in Mozambique alone. Because climate change is known to increase storm intensity over the Indian Ocean, some pointed out that Beira had a particular place in history: the first city to be completely destroyed by climate change.

I mention this because, while the media didn't exactly ignore cyclone Idai, Beira is hardly a household name. Idai didn't feature in end-of-year round-ups of 2019. It didn't make CNN's top 100 stories of the year, which was topped by the fire at Notre Dame in Paris.[14] The first city to be annihilated by climate change barely left a mark.

Would Beira be remembered if its citizens were White?

The proximity problem

When I was a journalism student, the question of what makes something newsworthy was one of the first topics we covered. Proximity is one factor: an incident nearby is more disturbing than one far away. In 2017 I strolled across Westminster Bridge to a meeting at the Houses of Parliament. Almost exactly 24 hours later, an attacker ploughed a 4×4 into pedestrians on that bridge. This kind of proximity triggers the chilling thought that 'it could have been me', or 'there but for the grace of God, go I'.

Proximity is psychological as well as geographical. New Zealand is as far from Britain as you can get, but British news viewers were still shocked by the Christchurch shootings. 51 people were killed at mosques on 25 March 2019, on the same day that cyclone Idai hit Beira.

The running order for the evening news is not calculated on the basis of whose pain is greatest. It's a complex and subjective balancing of relevance, novelty and many other things – and so it should be. But there is a pattern to what news editors focus on and what they miss. In Chapter 2 I mentioned the list of the most under-reported crises of 2019. Nine out of ten of them were in Africa and involved Black suffering. The other was in North Korea, which is notoriously difficult to report on.[15]

The attention different countries command isn't just to do with disasters and tragedy either. Remember that survey from the Commonwealth Games from Chapter 5? The same survey asked people which countries they most wanted to see succeed at the Games, other than Britain. Of the 77 participating countries, the top three were Australia, New Zealand and Canada. These just happen to be the only three countries in the Games that are both English-speaking and White.[16]

When it comes to news, people are naturally more interested in people like them. They care more about those with similar lifestyles, language or skin colour. They are easier to relate to. When a big story breaks in a developing country, often the White people involved become the focus – a British nurse who contracts Ebola, the European holidaymakers caught up in a tsunami.

This difference in how we relate and empathise creates an unspoken hierarchy of shock and concern. 'Different countries are assigned different value,' as the Ernman-Thunberg family put it in their book *Our House Is on Fire*. 'Citizens in different countries are seen to be of different worths. Or at least different newsworthiness. But it can't be ruled out that the newsworthiness infects other values. Such as human values.'[17]

Compassion fatigue

It's impossible to care about everything all the time. Everybody has their own life to live. 'You told yourself you'd be attuned to a holocaust unfolding a world away, but you weren't,' a character muses to themselves in Rumaan Alam's novel *Leave the World Behind*. 'Terrible things happened constantly and never prevented you from going out for ice cream.'[18]

Climate disaster might feel like a world away, but our shared global atmosphere makes distance an illusion. Careless lives in consumer cultures are responsible for those fires and floods and droughts. Through their high carbon footprints, the citizens of the global North – especially the polluter elite – are complicit in disasters such as Beira's destruction. It is the greenhouse gases of the richest that warm the climate and feed those stronger hurricanes.

The damage caused by the climate emergency happens a long way from where it is generated. It happens in places that White news viewers struggle to relate to, and among people with whom they do not empathise.

Climate suffering is not going anywhere. There is more to come, and it will continue to feature Black and Brown suffering. As it goes on, another risk presents itself: will audiences become numb to it? What little feeling there might have been for the far-flung victims of the climate crisis may erode as the years pass, as compassion fatigue sets in.

Will the injustices of climate change be added to the pile of racial injustices that didn't stop us 'going out for ice cream' – alongside sweatshop labour, unfair trade rules, refugee crises or global waste dumping? It would be, unfortunately, par for the course. 'Callous disregard for lives that are not White,' writes

Kehinde Andrews, 'has been the defining feature of Western development.'[19]

All of this is a major obstacle to climate justice.

Rebuilding empathy

When I first started reading about the empathy gap, I wondered whether it was better left out of the book. It could easily be used as an excuse. If people are hard-wired to respond more to people who are like them, how can anyone criticise them for caring less about the suffering of people of colour?

Then I came across a finding that surprised me: Black people show the same empathy gap. Where Black participants were included in the experiment, they too had less of a response to Black suffering.

This would suggest that the empathy gap is culturally learned. It is not inherent, not biological or embedded in genetics. It is more to do with perceptions and assumptions of value, rather than a natural ability to relate to people who are different from us.

People seem to think that those with low status can handle more pain because they have experienced more of it. 'Because Blacks have relatively low status in US society,' say the researchers, 'people may assume that Black people have less privileged lives – lives with more hardships – and infer that they must be tougher.'[20]

To put it another way, the empathy gap is itself a product of racism.

Racism can be internalised, writes the African American political scientist Terri Givens, leading to a situation where 'Black people often lack empathy for themselves and for each other.'[21]

If the empathy gap is cultural, then it is not inevitable. Change is possible. As the philosopher Roman Krznaric demonstrates in his book on the topic, empathy can be nurtured and its scope can be expanded. It may turn out to be vital to the struggle. Climate justice may depend on 'imagining ourselves into the lives and thoughts of the current and future victims of global warming'.[22]

Change is in the air already, through movements such as Black Lives Matter that affirm the value of the Black experience, and demand equality and dignity. As these messages gain ground, society may be able to cultivate greater empathy and understanding, eroding both prejudice and compassion fatigue. It is towards these sorts of solutions that we can now turn.

Representation

In May 2020, an African American man named Christian Cooper was birdwatching in Central Park. He was in an area called The Ramble, which is kept wild and where ground-dwelling birds can be found. A White woman came through with her dog, which was running free despite the signs saying that this was forbidden. Concerned for the birds, Cooper asked the woman to put her dog back on the lead. She refused, the conversation escalated, and she ended up calling the police. 'I'm going to tell them there's an African American man threatening my life,' she shouted as she made the call. Cooper captured the whole conversation on film, and the footage went viral.[1]

In response, a collective of Black naturalists launched Black Birders Week. Using the hashtag #BlackInNature, thousands of Black birdwatchers posted pictures and introduced themselves on social media. Stories were exchanged. 'Ask a Black Birder' question-and-answer sessions were organised on Twitter. Connections were made between birders in America, the Caribbean, Africa and beyond. A crowdfunding campaign was launched to buy binoculars for young Black birders. And there were many, many pictures of birds.

'Black Birders Week really aims to create a space where Black people can be visible,' said one of the organisers, PhD student Juita Martinez, 'and to let everyone out there know that there are systematic barriers, especially racism, that can prevent Black people from utilizing these spaces and enjoying birds, like everyone else who isn't Black might be enjoying them.'[2]

The importance of representation

Looking out the window right now I can see six swifts and a pigeon. I can hear sparrows and a blackbird, and the chattery alarm call of a magpie. Sometimes I look up and see red kites soaring overhead. They nest in the grounds of the water tower on the other side of the road.

It would never have occurred to me that racism could interfere with someone's appreciation of birds. The definition of White privilege is to be ignorant of racism, and I did not realise that White privilege could apply to birdwatching. As participants in Black Birder Week repeatedly showed, there are racial obstacles to enjoying nature. Many shared stories of how they were viewed suspiciously when on reserves or out with their binoculars. Some had been approached by the police or by rangers to ask them what they were doing, even though they were doing exactly the same thing as the White birdwatchers.

In his autobiography *The Home Place: Memoirs of a Colored Man's Love Affair with Nature*, the biologist J. Drew Lanham describes being followed while at work, or finding the letters KKK spray-painted at one of his study sites. One research job required him to count birds as part of an annual census, which meant driving round and parking up to watch and make notes. This was fine in the countryside but also included counting birds in White suburban neighbourhoods – a simple task for a White person, but a much riskier activity for a Black scientist.[3]

There are intersectional aspects to this as well, where racial inequality meets the male-oriented culture of the outdoors. 'The visibility of Black women who bird is really not out there,' said Deja Perkins, an urban ecologist and organiser of Black Birders Week. 'We don't really see representation of ourselves in this activity, so I think it's really important for us to highlight that women are out here birding.'[4]

Black Birder Week is a positive and empowering reaction to a racist incident, and it demonstrates the importance of representation. Raising the visibility of Black birders made me aware of a form of racial discrimination that I didn't know about. It prompts nature reserves and national parks to review their operations to make sure they do not reinforce these inequalities. And it builds solidarity in the Black birding community, legitimising and encouraging more people to take part, when nature appreciation has not been seen as part of Black culture.*

_____

* For similar initiatives in Britain, see Black2Nature, founded by teenage nature enthusiast Mya-Rose Craig; Black Girls Hike UK; Wild in the City; Kit Collective.

Not my place

As an activist, almost every group I have ever been part of has struggled with questions of diversity. They have all been 'too White'. All of them have been well aware of that, and none of them has known what to do about it. It is not enough to keep the door open, to insist that everyone is welcome. Movements like Black Birder Week highlight how deep the difficulties go.

Dorceta Taylor, one of America's most respected environmental justice scholars, describes how 'racial and ethnic minorities are often viewed as lacking interest in and concern for the environment'.[5] Her research reveals that to be a stereotype. Black participants in her studies say they feel connected to nature and are curious about it, and their fears and dislikes don't wildly differ from White participants'. Where there are differences in engagement with nature, she argues the reasons are more likely to be found in class, education, culture and opportunity – not in race. We saw in Chapter 7 how, in America, levels of concern about the climate are higher among people of colour.

Activist networks might lament the lack of diversity, but there are obstacles to engaging with nature that White people might not know about. There are economic barriers, as ethnic minority communities are concentrated in urban areas. People of colour may have less access to wild places and feel less welcome when they do visit. This creates the perception that nature and the environment is not for them. That can become embedded in culture and reinforced through peer pressure.

'No adults and no kids were into nature,' says the writer and photographer Dudley Edmondson, who was laughed at as a child for his interests. 'I was literally the only person of colour that was into nature and the environment. I didn't have any role models.' It's a perception he worked to change with the ground-breaking photographic book *The Black & Brown Faces in America's Wild Places*, published in 2006. 'Nature isn't just for White people. It never has been, though it may appear to be.'[6]

I felt this myself on a visit to the Lake District recently, a famously beautiful area in the North of England. Accustomed to the multicultural streets of Luton, I couldn't help but notice that visitors to its villages and trails were 99 per cent White people in expensive primary-coloured jackets. It made me uncomfortable, even as a White person in an expensive jacket. For Ingrid Pollard, a founding member of the Association of Black Photographers, that feeling would have been greatly multiplied. All her life she had heard how inspiring they were, 'but when I went to the Lakes myself, I found I kind of wanted to hide behind a bush'.[7]

I don't say this to make anyone feel bad for being White in the Lakes, but to highlight how a landscape with real cultural resonance can be experienced in very different ways by someone of colour. 'It's as if the Black experience is only lived within an urban environment,' Pollard writes. 'A visit to the countryside is always accompanied by a feeling of unease.' Her portraits of Black people in the Lake District, taken in 1988, are held in the collections of the Victoria and Albert Museum.[8]

Representation is about faces, bodies, people – knowing that I belong because there are others like me here. It is also about ideas and perspectives, the stories that are told about why the environment matters and what climate change is all about. And there are problems here too.

White bookshelves

I recently compiled a list of the top 50 books on climate change, cross-referencing the US and UK bestseller lists across the climate and environment categories of a handful of book websites. The big hitters are all there – Naomi Klein's *This Changes Everything*, David Wallace-Wells' *The Uninhabitable Earth*, Greta Thunberg's collected speeches. Al Gore. Bill McKibben. There are some climate sceptic titles among them too.

Here's the author breakdown of those books: out of the 50, two are co-authored. Among the named authors are 42 men and eight women. 49 are White, and one is Asian.

The Asian entry into the top 50 is the Indian novelist Amitav Ghosh, with his book *The Great Derangement: Climate Change and the Unthinkable*. He argues that the debate around climate change is too Eurocentric. It has focused on the views of Europe and the nations settled by Europeans, and he encourages his readers to 'look at the climate crisis through the prism of empire'.

He explains how Asia's responsibility for climate change is fundamentally different from the West's. The West's contribution is based on the long and slow growth in the carbon footprint of their populations, taking place over centuries. 'Asia's contribution, on the other hand, came about through a sudden but very small expansion in the footprint of a much larger number of people.'[9]

The Empire is one of the reasons for this. As we saw in Chapter 5, colonial authorities held back development in their overseas territories. The industrial technologies that were coming out of Britain were quickly taken up in other European countries but not in the colonies. The Empire wanted India to be a provider of raw materials, not a manufacturer. 'The emerging fossil-fuel economies of the West required that people elsewhere be prevented from developing coal-based energy systems of their own.'[10]

India's emissions have rocketed skywards in recent decades in part because industrialisation had been suppressed and delayed under the Empire. When Western commentators blame Asia for climate change, they are writing empire out of the story.

They may also miss the sense of betrayal involved. Having followed the West's path and adopted fossil fuels and industry, it is only now apparent that it's an impossible dream. 'Every family in the world cannot have two cars, a washing machine, and a refrigerator,' writes Ghosh, 'not because of technical or economic limitations but because humanity would asphyxiate in the process.'[11]

India was denied industry, then encouraged to industrialise, only to realise that the powers of empire have used up the carbon budget — and still want to blame Asia for climate change.

This post-colonial perspective is not widely represented in Western debates around the climate. But if slavery, colonialism and empire are whitewashed out of the picture — something Britain unfortunately excels at — then it is easy to look at current emissions on their own and see Asia as a climate pariah. Politicians and tabloid journalists then make sweeping statements about Asian responsibility which, to Asian eyes, may come across as imperialist and racist. Politicians or diplomats may go into international negotiations viewing countries such as India as obstinate polluters. International agreements have stalled on such claims in the past, and global cooperation is impossible without understanding how history affects climate justice.

But Ghosh's is the only book by a person of colour in the top 50.

Voices from the margins

In the dominance of White male perspectives in climate change literature, what else are we missing? I write as one myself, so it's not that White males have nothing to say. But I suspect that the climate change debate would be less concerned with numbers, technologies, targets and competing national interests if there were fewer White men round the table. Perhaps a wider conversation would find more room for cooperation, equity, solidarity, commons approaches, natural solutions, communities, well-being, consensus building, the reality of suffering and the need for global justice.*

There are some very common ideas in environmental circles that can sound very different when viewed from a non-Western perspective. For example, the climate crisis is often described as a *global* catastrophe. It's there in phrases such as 'all in the same boat', as if humanity were the Titanic striking the iceberg of climate change.

Asad Rehman, a Pakistani-born British campaigner, describes the problem with this global catastrophe narrative:

'We may all be on the Titanic, but it's the rich, White industrialised countries who are on the top deck, sipping their cocktails, listening to the orchestra and waiting for some technological fix to save them, whilst in the hold of the Titanic are Black, Brown, Indigenous people, poor Brown and Black people from the Global South, who are already drowning, and when they try and flee, they find that the escape hatch is bolted.'[12]

* For a great demonstration of this, see *All We Can Save*, edited by Ayana Elizabeth Johnson and Katharine K. Wilkinson — a collection of essays by women in the climate movement, and one of my favourite climate books.

It is obviously true that we are all on the one planet, and it is true that climate change will affect everyone eventually. It is the dominance of this perspective that is the problem, the way that it becomes a default way of speaking about the climate crisis. To put everyone 'in it together' puts everyone on an equal footing, and that obscures the reality of Black and Brown suffering today.

Activists in comfortable parts of the Earth, such as myself, might see 'in it together' as a statement of solidarity. But I am not up to my arms in mud. What looks like solidarity to me may be hollow words to someone who is suffering now in a more vulnerable part of the world.

Asad Rehman points out the problems with another common theme in the environmental movement, that of protecting future generations. Inter-generational injustice is real, and the school strikers have articulated this with powerful moral clarity. However, 'it makes tackling climate change something to be achieved in the future, because that's when it's about saving our grandchildren, our great-grandchildren,' says Rehman. 'But from a climate justice perspective, this crisis is not about tomorrow, or about our future generations. Talking about future generations marginalises the reality of impacts today. It says that Black Lives Don't Matter as much as the lives of White European children.'[13]

Again, it is not wrong to be stirred into action on behalf of future generations. But if this becomes a central and dominant narrative, the voices that are pushed to the margins are the same ones that are always pushed away.

'Environmental issues'

Perhaps one of the trickiest aspects of environmentalism is the idea of the environment itself.

Ask children to draw a picture to represent climate change, and a fair percentage of them are likely to include a blue globe with a green and dubious approximation of the continents. (This is despite the fact that not all the continents are green, and I will let you reflect on that in your own time.)

You may also find penguins, coral reefs, polar bears, maybe a rainforest. Often the penguins are crying or holding up a sign saying 'help'. Human figures are rare.* Plenty of pictures like this have been drawn on the dining table in my own home, and it's not the children's fault. This is how environmental issues are taught. A quick look at the School Resources page of WWF at the time of writing reveals a picture of a polar bear and an image of the Earth rendered entirely in blue and green.[14]

Plenty of environmentalists understand the problem with these messages, and many organisations have made a conscious decision to move away from imagery of melting ice and polar bears. Nevertheless, they are deeply embedded in the public imagination. From an early age, climate change is mentally categorised as an environmental issue, to do with nature and animals more than people and justice. Children learn that climate change is bad because it makes animals sad.

---

* You can see over a thousand children's drawings of climate change at www.kidscareaboutclimate.org

As adults, people still navigate environmental issues through the prism of wildlife. Nothing happened when the entire city of Beira in Mozambique was flattened by a cyclone, but millions of British TV viewers were mobilised by the sight of a turtle with a straw stuck in its nose.

I saw that programme too, and no plastic straw shall touch my lips again. I get it. Of course we should care for nature and for wildlife, which is indeed being devastated by human activity right now. A love for nature is often a gateway into environmental activism, and that is true for people of colour as much as it is for White folks. But that is not enough, not if we truly aspire to build a global sense of unity around climate change.

Imagine how people in Beira might see the Western environmental movement – would they see their experience of climate change represented?

Too White

When critics say 'the climate movement is too White', the skin colour of the crowd is an indicator of the problem, not the problem itself. Just addressing the colour is what leads to tokenism, when everybody can point to the Asian in the room and congratulate themselves on being inclusive. The deeper problem is the dominance of White thinking, environmentalism from a place of privilege, Western framings of the crisis.

Yes, there aren't enough Black and Brown faces in the crowd. Perhaps that is because the movement may not be asking the right questions or telling the right stories. If certain communities don't see their concerns or priorities addressed, they may focus their efforts elsewhere.

'I felt very left out of it,' says Mary Annaïse Heglar, describing her first engagement with the climate change movement. As someone who had lived through Hurricane Katrina first-hand, the usual environmental narratives felt shallow – 'like they're coming from people who have never had to fight for their lives before'.[15]

Everyone has limited time and energy to give to activism, and people of colour may feel forced to choose between the environmental movement or civil rights action. 'How can we expect Black Americans to focus on climate when we are so at risk on our streets, in our communities, and even within our own homes?' asks the climate scientist Ayana Elizabeth Johnson. 'I would love to ignore racism and focus all my attention on climate. But I can't. Because I am human. And I'm Black.'[16]

When the conversation is dominated by White men, the debate can be skewed towards their priorities and preoccupations. A debate with more women, more racial diversity, more indigenous people, will be richer and more effective. It would be more alert to racism, to justice, and the many ways that people of colour are excluded. Paying attention to representation requires a deliberate effort to seek out alternative voices, to listen, and to amplify those causes rather than simply recruit for our own. This is true not just of environmentalism of course, but of politics, art, popular culture and society at large.

Black and Brown lives are at risk from climate change. If the climate movement wants to communicate that these lives matter, then it will have to show that Black questions matter, Black ideas, Black imaginations, stories, perspectives, and experiences.

10

Doing justice

'Climate change, which was largely brought about by the activities of developed countries, has made it difficult for poor and vulnerable countries to fight poverty,' wrote Meles Zenawi in 2009. It was the run-up to the international climate change talks in Copenhagen, and the Prime Minister of Ethiopia was seen as a leading African voice on climate. 'No amount of money will undo the damage done. But adequate investment in mitigating the damage could partly resolve the problem.'[1]

The 53 members of the African Union had chosen Zenawi to lead a delegation to the Copenhagen talks, with the express purpose of putting climate justice on the agenda. Besides Antarctica, they argued, Africa was the only continent that had not yet industrialised. It had contributed the least to climate change, and would be hit the hardest. That injustice needed to be addressed, and the chairman of the African Union, the Gabonese diplomat Jean Ping, had a clear solution in mind: 'Africa must be compensated by developed countries for the impact of climate change.'[2]

On a public relations blitz ahead of the conference, Zenawi set out the message from Africa. They would be negotiating as a bloc, and they wanted 1.5 degrees of warming as a target. Agreements needed to be legally binding. They would be insisting on compensation, and they would not accept a token sum. A realistic figure would be much higher, but at the minimum they would be seeking a 'conservative' $50 billion a year in 2015, increasing to $100 by 2020.

The global North was 'morally obliged to pay partial compensation to poor and vulnerable countries', Zenawi wrote in the *Guardian* newspaper. 'If the developed world is able to pay trillions of dollars to clean up its bankers' mess, how is it possible that it cannot afford to pay billions of dollars to clean up a mess that it created, and that is threatening the survival of whole continents?'[3]

Betrayal

Three weeks later, the rhetoric had changed. As the talks faltered, France issued a communiqué agreed with Ethiopia – President Sarkozy was apparently speaking for Africa now. The new position called for a target of two degrees and did not include legally binding emissions cuts from developed countries. The proposed compensation amounted to a mere $10 billion a year. Since the African Union had voted to let Zenawi negotiate for everyone, that was the end of Africa's demands.

African delegates rounded on Zenawi, who had been elected in good faith to represent agreed bottom lines. 'If Prime Minister

Meles wants to sell out the lives and hopes of Africans for a pittance, he is welcome to, but that is not Africa's position,' said Mithika Mwenda, a Kenyan representative of the Pan-African Climate Justice Alliance. His colleague Augustine Njamnshi, a lawyer from Cameroon, was equally blunt: 'You cannot say you are proposing a "solution" to climate change if your solution will see millions of Africans die and if the poor, not the polluters, keep paying for climate change.'[4]

What lay behind this betrayal? President Sarkozy of France had obviously been influential. The White House had announced that President Obama had phoned Zenawi. Had he been bought? Zenawi died in 2012 and the truth may never be known. What is known is that Western diplomats used promises of aid and funding to erode resolve and get countries to agree to a compromise.[5] The cache of US embassy files that was released by Wikileaks in 2010 documents several instances. A meeting between US and EU officials discussed how to 'work around unhelpful countries' and 'neutralise, co-opt or marginalise' those who didn't want to sign the negotiated agreement.[6] A memo describes a meeting with Zenawi where he is told that the US will need him to sign the Copenhagen Accord as a condition of further dialogue. Zenawi, in turn, mentions President Obama's 'personal assurance to him' of 'finances committed in Copenhagen'.[7]

Having looked at how post-colonialism operates in Chapter 5, there is no need to infer a conspiracy theory. This is how Western power has always operated: break up efforts at African unity, use aid as a bargaining chip, state the conditions you require for cooperation. The Copenhagen talks were widely seen as a failure, but the Western nations got the accord they wanted – one with no legal obligations and that did not recognise the ecological debt they owed to Africa. Compensation for climate change was successfully removed from international debate.

Failing to act

Climate justice was elbowed off the agenda in Copenhagen and remained a minor theme in international talks. There were some concessions to recognising the 'loss and damage' of climate change in later talks and the creation of a Green Climate Fund to disburse funds to help vulnerable countries adapt. But this came with no obligations and remains severely underfunded. Of the money that is disbursed through the fund, most of it goes to mitigation, not adaptation. Mohamed Adow, director of the Kenya-based think tank Power Shift Africa, observes that 'although rich countries want to stop poor countries from emitting greenhouse gases, they have shown less interest in protecting those countries' people and property'.[8]

The Paris Agreement, negotiated six years after Copenhagen, scrupulously avoids any sense of climate justice. The term gets one passing mention in the preamble: 'noting the importance for some of the concept of "climate justice"'. Every word is argued over in an agreement like this. The 'noting' 'for some' and the inverted commas will have been specially requested to dial down the significance of the term even making an appearance.[9]

The compromise of the Paris Agreement was to make carbon reductions voluntary. Each country could decide for itself how far and how fast it would reduce its destruction of the Earth's life support systems. Five years later, analysis by Climate Action Tracker showed that out of 197 signatories just six had made voluntary pledges that would be compatible with two degrees of warming, India among them. Only two countries have made pledges for 1.5 degrees: Morocco and The Gambia. None of these eight climate leaders is a developed country, or majority White. Half of them are in Africa.[10]

Despite some positive steps by developed countries, especially within the EU, progress is slow. For many of the countries dragging their heels, there is no great urgency – the prerogative of the climate-privileged. The consequences are out of sight and out of mind, but real nonetheless. Every delay is paid for in Black suffering.

By now it should be clear what this means for climate policy-making. In the words of Ibram X. Kendi, founder of the Center for Antiracist Research at Boston University: 'Do-nothing climate policy is racist policy, since the predominantly non-White global South is being victimised by climate change more than the Whiter global North, even as the Whiter global North is contributing more to its acceleration.'[11]

Reparations

If climate change is a form of structural racism, then perhaps there are parallels with calls for reparations elsewhere, such as slavery in the United States. Robert L. Johnson became the first African American billionaire when he sold his network, Black Entertainment Television, in 2000. In 2020 he wrote: 'The only way to unify this nation and achieve racial equality and harmony is for this country to implement full and total economic reparations in the form of direct cash payments, over the next 10 to 20 years, to every descendent of African American slaves.'[12]

Johnson was adding his voice to a debate that has been rolling for 200 years, ever since the United States ended slavery without compensating the slaves for their lost labour. To that original sin came segregation, red-lining, voter suppression and many other discriminatory practices.

Ending the abuse is not enough. Even if all discrimination could be ended today, the damage would still be done. 'If you stick a knife in my back nine inches and pull it out six inches, there's no progress,' as the civil rights leader Malcolm X said in an interview in 1964. 'If you pull it all the way out that's not progress. Progress is healing the wound that the blow made.'[13]

There is another parallel in reparations for empire. 'Britain's rise for 200 years was financed by its depredations in India,' the Indian Parliamentarian Dr Shashi Tharoor told the Oxford Union Society in a debate on reparations. One recent study attempted to put a figure on this plunder and estimated that Britain extracted some $45 trillion in wealth from India during the colonial era.[14] It's a colossal sum, but the impossibility of a full repayment of the debt shouldn't end the discussion.

Accepting responsibility is an important first step: 'What is required,' says Tharoor, 'is accepting the principle that reparations are owed.'[15]

That first step is hard enough. The issue came up in 2015 on an official visit to Jamaica by then Prime Minister David Cameron. Barbadian historian Sir Hilary Beckles wrote to Cameron ahead of the visit to say: 'You owe it to us as you return here to communicate a commitment to reparatory justice that will enable your nation to play its part in cleaning up this monumental mess of Empire.'[16] Cameron would not hear of it, leaving it to his spokesperson to say simply that 'he wants to focus on the future'.[17]

Focusing on the future is the reply of the privileged. For those still living with historic disadvantage, the ancestors of the plundered rather than the plunderers, it's no answer at all. The injustice remains, and there are active reparations campaigns around the oppression of indigenous communities, genocide, forced displacement, colonialism and more besides.

These are long-running campaigns and fraught with complexity, but some have been successful. In 2008 Italy became the first to compensate a former colony, signing a treaty of friendship with Libya. Certain indigenous groups have won compensation in New Zealand and Canada. In Chapter 5, I mentioned the slave-owning founder of the pub chain Greene King. In 2020 the company apologised for its history and promised to 'make a substantial investment to benefit the BAME community'.[18] Lloyds of London, which used to insure slave ships on the trans-Atlantic trade routes, made a similar statement on the same day. A public relations exercise, some might say, but it at least acknowledges the debt. That in itself is a step in the right direction.

Climate compensation

The big difference between these examples and climate change is that reparations are to make up for a historic wrong. Climate change is a product of past emissions, but it is also happening now, and current actions will determine how bad it will be. It isn't something I can blame on my ancestors for being racist imperialists. I am implicated right now in the breakdown of the climate and how it affects people of colour around the world.

In that sense, the climate change struggle is closer to the abolition movement than it is to reparations campaigns. It is not just making up for past wrongs, but preventing suffering now. To borrow Malcolm X's metaphor, the stabbing has to stop before the healing can begin.

That is strong language, but it is important to understand that climate change is a matter of life and death. The latest IPCC report details the effects of climate change on Africa, a continent that is warming faster than the global average. It forecasts a reduction in rainfall in large parts of the continent and greatly increased water stress. Heat and water shortages will affect agriculture, reducing yields and increasing food insecurity in regions already prone to drought and famine. Disease lines are moving, exposing more people to risk from malaria and other diseases.[19]

To the African experience we can add the damage to Pakistan, India, Bangladesh, small island states, the Caribbean, Central America, and marginalised communities throughout the world. The increased risks of climate breakdown are falling on some of the world's poorest, with the fewest resources to protect themselves or to rebuild when disaster strikes.

When countries act to address their emissions, or choose not to, they are making decisions about which places will survive to the end of the 21st century and which places will be abandoned, which cultures will thrive and which ones will be annihilated. It's the politics of who lives and who dies – 'necropolitics', as the Cameroonian philosopher Achille Mbembe calls it.[20]

Climate finance – support for adapting to a changing world – is about survival. It saves lives. It is about averting ecocide.

Restorative justice

Fania Davis is a civil rights attorney, born in the segregated South and a lifelong race campaigner (as is her well-known sister, Angela Davis). She argues that restorative justice could be applied to many of America's race problems, from school exclusions to mass incarceration or police brutality. It is an approach that offers 'the possibility of recognizing, taking responsibility for, and repairing harm, both interpersonal and structural'.[21]

Restorative justice is different from 'retributive justice', which seeks to punish. Through a prison sentence, a fine or a physical punishment, retributive justice ensures that the perpetrator suffers some form of harm or deprivation. This is supposed to make up for the crime, acts as a deterrent to others, and forms the basis for most Western justice systems today.[22]

Restorative justice, on the other hand, focuses on putting things right. While there may still be serious consequences for serious crimes, the overall ethos is to value healing rather than punishment, and not to return harm for harm. In a restorative process, victims and perpetrators enter into a dialogue with skilled mediators. Through mutual understanding, there can be apology and perhaps forgiveness. Restitution can be made. Losses can be paid back. There is closure and the possibility of moving on.

When thinking about justice for multi-generational wrongs such as slavery, empire or climate change, retributive justice is no use at all. It would not be ethical to attempt to 'punish' White people today for the crimes of their ancestors. There cannot be justice through retribution, piling harm upon harm. But perhaps there can be restoration.

Guilt and healing

An important aspect of restorative justice is that it seeks healing on both sides. 'What is needed is an airing of family secrets, a settling with old ghosts,' writes the essayist Ta-Nehisi Coates in his influential article 'The Case for Reparations'. 'What is needed is a healing of the American psyche and the banishment of White guilt.'[23] This would not be a matter of paying off Black communities to make them go away. It would be a moment of 'national reckoning that would lead to spiritual renewal'.

The Germans, you will not be surprised to learn, have a word for this: *Vergangenheitsbewältigung*, learning from and reckoning with a difficult past.

I see the harm of colonialism and racist oppression stretching back into history, and the destruction of the climate crisis stretching into the future, always the same people coming out on top and the same people exploited. I want justice for those who have been robbed and for those who suffer. I want a secure future for the African island nation I once called home. I also want to make peace with my own country and its legacy. I long for an end to denial, for the renewal that Coates describes.

I can hear my little pink children giggling in the garden. I want it for them. If my generation does not honestly confront the past and take responsibility for structural racism, it will fall to theirs. They will have enough to deal with already.

I do not know the detail of what a restorative justice process might look like for climate change, but the call for reparations will circle around again. How that might be organised would be a whole book in itself, but perhaps we can see some starting points. For instance, a restorative justice approach would need truth-telling and a recognition of past wrongs. There may need to be a Truth and Reconciliation Commission for climate change, learning from what South Africa and a number of other countries have done to redress the legacy of racist policies or dictatorships.

To make a lasting difference, restorative justice projects would need to build inclusion, rather than seeking one-off attempts at compensation – not least because the debt that is owed is so large that it is fundamentally unpayable. This inclusion could be grounded in practical benefits such as community energy, reforestation and land restoration – all underpinned by significant emissions cuts in developed countries.

One thing I do know is that this kind of restorative justice begins at the intersection: with a meeting of respective movements, recognising that race and the environment cannot be separated. That is what we will look at next.

11

Common cause

November 2015, the week before the crucial climate talks begin in Paris. They are seen by many as a last chance to secure an international agreement on climate change, and climate marches are held around the world. I had planned to join the march in Paris and report from the talks – my Eurostar ticket and hostel accommodation were booked. The terrorist attacks in Paris put an end to that, and I took the train to London instead.

I travelled with my son Zach, aged four at the time. It was the first time I'd taken him to a big march, and he was buzzing with energy. From his point of view it was largely a forest of legs, and I hoisted him onto my shoulders so he could see what 70,000 people looked like. My father-in-law had come down from Shrewsbury on a coach, and we found him in the crowd and the drizzle. And then we waited.

There was a long delay before we set off, but we were some distance from the front and didn't know why. People got tired of holding their placards, many of them in the shape of hearts with the words 'for the love of...' on them and a space for people to fill in what they were marching to protect. Around us I read 'my grandchildren', 'trees', and somewhat bizarrely, 'for the love of dogs'. People put down their banners, and then sat on the tarmac.

Later I found out what had caused the hold-up.

After months of negotiation, it had been agreed that a coalition called Wretched of the Earth would lead the march. They are an alliance of frontline and indigenous communities who are suffering the effects of climate change and fossil fuel extraction.* Members from the Sámi people of Scandinavia and Pacific Islanders had travelled to take part. But when it came to the day itself, the organisers got cold feet. Wretched of the Earth unfurled a large banner reading 'Still fighting CO2onialism' and a sign saying 'British imperialism causes climate injustice'.

This was not on-brand. It clashed with the more universal messages of the 'for the love of' campaign, which had been carefully focus-grouped to bring more positivity to the event.[1] Right before the march was due to set off, the organisers hurried a group of marchers in animal costumes down a side street and round to the front. They unfurled a different banner and posed for the press. The Wretched of the Earth bloc sat down

* The name is taken from Frantz Fanon's 1961 book on neo-colonialism, *The Wretched of the Earth*.

in protest and refused to move, and, until it was all sorted out, thousands of people behind them waited in the rain and wondered about the delay.

Diversity and inclusion

In an open letter after the event, Wretched of the Earth pointed out the tragedy of the moment:

'The place of indigenous, Black and Brown people was stolen and given away to people dressed as animals. This is colonialism at its most basic and obvious. The history of conquest, genocide, and slavery is the foundation of our modern economic system – the very system responsible for the global disaster that is climate change. This is the same history that compares Indigenous, Black and Brown people to animals and treats them as such.'[2]

Having ethnic minority marchers at the front was great for diversity, especially if indigenous people came in traditional costume. But if the expectation is that people of colour are seen and not heard, then they are being used – and that is no different from colonialism.

As Joshua Virasami and Alexandra Wanjiku Kelbert from the protest group Black Dissidents wrote about the incident, their presence at the march ticked the diversity box, bringing colour to proceedings. But what they wanted to see was a movement 'which doesn't compartmentalise the struggle into climate, racism, migration'. To be truly inclusive, the movement needed to be intersectional.[3]

Where is everybody?

Activist groups often recognise that they are unrepresentative and wish it were different. Groups I have been part of would talk about 'reaching out' to mosques or Black Pentecostal churches. And inevitably someone would ask: 'Where is the Black community? Why don't they care about the environment?'

As Chapter 9 described, it would be wrong to assume that Black and minority ethnic people don't care about the environment. For a start, White people are in the minority when it comes to global environmental action. All over the world, indigenous people, marginalised tribes and people of colour are fighting mines, dump sites, gas flaring, air and water pollution and any number of other environmental travesties. These are not 'greens' or environmentalists, but ordinary people trying to protect their land, water, lives and culture. The climate-privileged citizens of the temperate North might not be aware of these struggles, still casting climate change as primarily a threat to nature. (For the love of dogs, won't somebody think about the dogs?)

When people of colour look at environmental discourse, especially those from the diaspora of those frontline countries, they are unlikely to see their struggle represented. They may choose to put their energies elsewhere. That, in turn, makes those stories even less prominent, creating a vicious circle of narrowing interests.

Environmental justice is a factor here. As we saw in Chapter 3, people of colour are often closest to sources of pollution. That means that Black activists are more likely to have a local cause that demands their attention. 'African Americans, Black women – particularly Southern Black women – are no strangers to environmental activism,' says Heather McTeer Toney, the Mississippi-born senior advisor of the anti-pollution charity Moms Clean Air Force. 'Who exactly do you think is on the front lines every single day, fighting to keep our communities safe from industries, polluters, and those seeking to harm our kids?'[4]

Racism itself is another reason for the lack of diversity in environmental circles. The energy of Black and Brown communities is drawn into the struggle for recognition, for equality, for justice and an end to violence.

Climate activism is hard. It is emotionally draining. Burnout rates are high. I know many passionate activists who have had to step back to protect their mental health. If I were Black, I would have to carry this psychic weight at the same time as the burden of racism.

Using privilege

White privilege can allow people to ignore climate change because it doesn't affect them. Somewhat paradoxically, having the time and energy to devote to climate activism is also a privilege.

This isn't just about race. There are many forms of privilege that make some people better suited to certain actions.

Young people without children have different opportunities to those with families or care responsibilities. You can't get yourself arrested if you have to pick up the kids at half past three. On the other hand, some of the most radical activists I know are retired. 'We are often much more free than most people,' Phil Kingston told me, aged 83 and still regularly arrested for acts of civil disobedience for the climate. 'The consequences really don't matter in the same way.'[5]

A lot of activists understand this and talk about 'using their privilege'. For example, Extinction Rebellion (XR) trains people for non-violent direct action, and participants choose whether they will take part in an 'arrestable' or a supporting role. Though it is always a free choice, those without British citizenship are encouraged to choose supporting roles, as they could be deported if they get in trouble with the law. Likewise people of colour: White activists may feel safer with the police, and may be treated differently in the courts.

In a supportive critique of XR, the investigative journalist Nafeez Ahmed writes that people of colour would be 'inevitably marginalised by a movement whose principal focus is "disruption" actions premised on getting arrested'. Even though XR makes an effort to give a platform to minority voices, the photos in the press show White activists, and the iconic moments of arrest will usually involve White people. Leveraging privilege while people of colour play supporting roles might be well-meaning, but the effect is the same: 'erasing minorities and indigenous people from the movement'.[6]

When I, as a White person, attempt to use my privilege for good, I am still using something I shouldn't have. I am still benefiting from something that is inherently unfair. The White saviour complex lurks not far away: stand aside while the White people solve the problem on your behalf.

And yet it is absolutely right that White people step up and take action for the climate. It is White people who have been the main beneficiaries of the fossil fuel system and who most need to take responsibility.

This is something of a conundrum, and the way out of it is to pursue intersectional activism.

Sunrise

'I didn't identify with the climate movement,' writes Mattias Lehman, digital director of the Sunrise Movement and a Black resident of the Twin Cities, USA. 'I have always seen the climate movement as too White, too middle-class, and often more concerned with trees and polar bears than with the human destruction climate change wreaks disproportionately upon Black and Brown communities around the world.'

'The intersectionality of the Green New Deal is what brought me to Sunrise Movement, and it is what has brought so many people of colour into movements for climate justice, particularly the Indigenous movements that have always led the way.'[7]

Sunrise is an American youth-led movement that was formed to help more progressive political candidates to secure nominations, and then win elections. It has supported some of the country's most dynamic political voices, including congresswomen Alexandria Ocasio-Cortez and Ilhan Omar. The movement has always supported policies for social justice and for climate change side by side, including the radical vision for America contained in the Green New Deal.

The Green New Deal made climate justice explicit in ways that the UN process and most national legislation has shied away from. 'Climate change, pollution, and environmental destruction have exacerbated systemic racial, regional, social, environmental, and economic injustices,' reads the bill, 'disproportionately affecting indigenous peoples, communities of colour, migrant communities, deindustrialised communities, depopulated rural communities, the poor, low-income workers, women, the elderly, the unhoused, people with disabilities, and youth.'[8]

The Green New Deal has not been successful in the US, and neither was the candidacy of Sunrise-backed Bernie Sanders. Sunrise has nonetheless been highly influential, setting an agenda, changing people's expectations and drawing people of colour into the climate conversation. The influence of the Green New Deal is clearly visible in the climate policies of the Biden administration, which talks specifically about climate and environmental justice. It has inspired several other countries to introduce similar measures, including the EU and South Korea. Sunrise has already helped dozens of politicians into office, and as a youth movement, they have plenty of time. The Green New Deal was proposed as a ten-year project. Donald Trump may have to watch helplessly from his retirement bunker while they transform America.

Sunrise is perhaps the most high-profile intersectional movement in the world today, and it sums up many of the points I have argued in this book. 'This fight against climate change exists alongside the fight against White supremacy and colonialism,' reads the homepage of the Sunrise website. 'We see it in every pipeline that tears through Indigenous lands. We see it in every factory pumping pollutants into Black neighbourhoods. We see it in every cage at our borders imprisoning immigrants who tried to escape famine and drought.'[9]

This is what it looks like when a movement acknowledges the structural racism of climate change, and honours the experience of people of colour who are most affected by it.

Difficult connections

There is movement on all of these questions, and there has been progress. A growing number of groups recognise the need for social justice alongside environmental care. There was a positive shift in the late 2000s when aid and development organisations began to see that climate change was one of the biggest risks to ending poverty. The climate emergency could wipe out decades of development gains. Groups such as Oxfam, Christian Aid and Tearfund began to talk about the climate, and their involvement brought a real energy into the debate.

Having been part of some of these discussions, I know it has not been easy. Organisations have had to take their board members, staff and supporters on a journey, patiently making the case for climate action as part of their work. Many years of dedicated advocacy has gone into this shift already, and the journey is not complete yet. Supporters might now recognise the vulnerability of the poor communities they donate to, but might not have connected their plight with their own high-carbon lifestyles. They have been happy to take credit for the well that has been drilled, but not for the drought that made it necessary.

There's a jarring psychological jump here. If the charities and organisations were to point out the connection, Western charity supporters would go from the flattering role of the generous donor to realising they are complicit. They have been donating to relieve suffering that they have helped to cause. All of a sudden they aren't the hero of the story any more, and those donations start to look more like reparations.

That's a painful and humbling truth, and it would take a very brave charity to speak it. As one friend in the sector told me, when they mention carbon footprints and consumer lifestyles, 'that's when the big donors walk away'.

Getting intersectional

Despite its limits, the meeting of the development world and the climate world has been very productive, raising awareness of climate change as an issue of justice and economic inequality. Over a decade on, I think another moment of awakening is underway as climate and race come together.

There is a vibrant debate going on around these questions. Extinction Rebellion is considering adding some form of social justice element to its list of demands. Activist networks are organising race awareness seminars. Green organisations have issued statements in support of Black Lives Matter.

Leah Thomas is one of the young Black environmental leaders involved in these discussions. She had been frustrated that environmentalists were often motivated by future generations, or the suffering of endangered species, but apparently weren't motivated by the suffering of Black communities.

With a foot in both camps, Thomas saw the connection that others were missing: 'The systems of oppression that have led to the deaths of so many Black people were the same systems that perpetuated environmental injustice.' She saw the need for 'intersectional environmentalism' and started a project 'to introduce it into environmentalist dialogue – to spark conversation and mobilise the environmental community to be antiracist and not complicit'.[10]

Vanessa Nakate is another young activist who has highlighted the connection between race and climate. A pioneer of the youth strikes in Uganda, she experienced first-hand how African voices can be side-lined in international dialogue. She has become a powerful advocate for greater representation, and for awareness of how racism shapes the climate debate.

Intersectional environmentalism holds these struggles together. It stands with people of colour, and advocates for both people and planet.

Racism and class

Because it is alert to inequality in all its forms, intersectional environmentalism can help to overcome potential points of tension. That includes low-income White communities, where there can sometimes be resistance to antiracism and scepticism of privilege.

The Conservative MP for Mansfield, Ben Bradley, has been outspoken on this issue: 'I'd love those who speak about "white male privilege" to come to Mansfield to talk to the blokes who have spent their whole lives underground digging coal to keep our lights on, and who are now dying early of lung disease because of it.'[11]

Perhaps a better approach would be to go to Mansfield and swap stories about the many other ways that ordinary people have been failed by the fossil fuel industry. Former miners have paid a high price for coal power. So have the hurricane survivors of Haiti or Mozambique, or the residents of Port Arthur.

There is historical precedent for finding this kind of unity. During the Industrial Revolution, many saw a common cause between the working classes in the mills and the slaves on the plantations. The French Revolutionary government, having liberated the peasantry, abolished slavery across the French Empire in 1794: 40 years before the British Empire did the same.* They saw racism as an unacceptable 'aristocracy of the skin'.[12]

In Britain, working-class movements such as the Chartists backed abolition, while some of the country's earliest Black

---

* This act of emancipation is often forgotten because Napoleon – a shameless racist – would later overturn it.

activists advocated for democracy and workers' rights in the North of England. 'As a descendant of a West India slave,' the campaigner William Cuffay said in 1846, he was 'the friend of all who were struggling for freedom'.[13]

There is plenty that unites disenfranchised working-class White communities and disadvantaged Black communities across the world. Previous generations knew it, and future generations may well tap into that legacy. The fossil-fuelled capitalism that destroys the livelihoods of African farmers also wrings out and discards Mansfield miners. They have a common cause.

By throwing the concern for justice wide, intersectional activism can highlight these connections. It can forge new alliances that recognise racial and gender inequalities, but also geographical and economic divides.

The US Green New Deal, mentioned above, takes this approach and specifically includes de-industrialised towns alongside neglected Black neighbourhoods and Native American reserves. Early signs from the Biden presidency suggest that some lessons have been learned, with a new focus not just on climate change, but on its equity implications too. The administration has committed to reducing emissions, prioritising disadvantaged regions and 'delivering justice for communities who have been subjected to environmental harm'.[14]

Friends and allies

Intersectional environmentalism is going to mean more Black people at green rallies, and more green people at Black rallies.

But that doesn't mean that everybody needs to do everything. Intersectional activists do not get 25 hours in a day.

Neither is it wrong to be motivated by the plight of animals or damage to the natural world. Consider it an invitation to throw your sympathies wider, recognising that the same mindset that exploits nature exploits people too. The extractive forces of fossil-fuelled capitalism that destroy landscapes and habitats also destroy communities and cultures.

There is no need for competition, no hierarchy of causes. It is a shared struggle.

Alliances will work in both directions. 'The Black community in the US has faced an inability to breathe through both police violence and disproportionate impacts of poor air quality,' writes Leah Thomas, inviting Black Lives Matter activists into environmentalism.[15] At the same time, 'every environmentalist should be antiracist'.

Action for change is most powerful when it identifies common cause – pulling together antiracists, feminists, environmentalists and justice campaigners of all kinds, building unity, solidarity and strength in numbers.

And while I have talked about activists, organisations and movements in this chapter, the challenge of intersectionality is for everyone – for politicians, the media and for ordinary people trying to get on with their busy lives. Being an active and responsible citizen of the 21st century means being aware of climate change, inequality and race, and supporting movements for change across all of them. In the next and final chapter, I look at how to do that as individuals.

Living with the questions

The Brahmaputra River begins in the mountains of Tibet and flows through China, Bangladesh and India over the course of its 2,500-mile length. Its flow is seasonal and highly variable, water levels rising as the glaciers melt in the spring, and then again when the monsoon rains arrive in late summer. Climate change affects both of these hydrological events, melting more ice and increasing the intensity of the monsoons.

Floods have always been a part of life along the river, but climate change has made it much worse. The river burst its banks again in June of 2020, flooding over 2,000 villages and displacing a million people.[1] This time the floods came at the same time as the coronavirus pandemic.

Nandiram Payeng, a farmer in his fifties, knows what this is like. 'We had our houses, farms and cattle in our village,' he says of his experience several years before. 'But the river came and took everything away.'[2]

There are many factors in play along the Brahmaputra, including more people moving into the area than before. Flood walls to protect some areas have left others more vulnerable.

Nevertheless, climate change is taking people's homes, jobs and lives in India – people who have contributed almost nothing to global greenhouse gas concentrations. As explained in Chapter 6, this can be understood as an act of violence.

The high-carbon lifestyle of the world's elite, the majority of them White, causes devastating loss to others in more vulnerable parts of the world, mostly people of colour.

Consumers in the West are often told that they need to make sacrifices for the good of the climate – maybe to fly less or drive less or eat less meat. But a great many people are making sacrifices already. Their houses, cattle and farms have already been taken away. The key difference between them is that the sacrifices made in the West will mostly be voluntary, while the ones made in places like the Brahmaputra River Valley are involuntary.

Solidarity

There is a lot of discussion about the value of personal action for climate change. There are many campaigns and programmes encouraging people to make small lifestyle changes, offering top tips for reducing your carbon footprint. Then you get books like *The Uninhabitable Earth* by David Wallace-Wells, which takes a long existential stare into a worst-case climate scenario, and dismisses the idea of any lifestyle changes in response. Why would you, when the only things that will make a difference are going to be large-scale, system-wide changes?[3]

I don't think it's a question of whether people should make lifestyle changes or pursue political change. They should do both. In fact, lifestyle changes can be an important part of laying the groundwork for bigger things. The more people choose to give up their petrol car and drive an electric vehicle, the cheaper they become, the more charging infrastructure gets built, and the easier it becomes for governments to legislate to reduce oil consumption. Personal actions can model the change we want to see. They create market signals and build political support for wider change.

They also matter because of those involuntary sacrifices.

When I reduce my own carbon footprint, I can do so as an act of solidarity with those who are suffering. The American ethicist Kevin J. O'Brien, in his book *The Violence of Climate Change*, suggests that 'the best way for privileged people to help liberate such people from involuntary sacrifices is by making our own voluntary sacrifices'.[4]

As I have argued throughout this book, climate change is structurally racist and is essentially perpetrated against people of colour. Reducing my carbon footprint is part of an appropriate response to that. Taking responsibility for my carbon footprint acknowledges that climate change causes Black suffering. I acknowledge my complicity in that racist structure, and I will work to dismantle it and reduce my involvement in it.

I can say that Black lives matter. I can take the knee as a symbolic gesture. But when I get in my car or fly on a plane, I contribute to a global injustice that considers Black lives cheap. My actions don't match my words. And while I cannot extricate myself from this injustice entirely, I have a responsibility to do what I can.

Taking responsibility

When I do interviews or panel discussions on climate change, there's a question that is almost guaranteed to feature: 'What are three simple things that people can do to reduce their carbon footprint?' If I am given the questions in advance, I ask why that one has been included. The answer from the moderator is usually that many people don't know what they could do, and there is lot of confusion about what makes a real difference.

That may be true, but every adult in Britain has seen suggestions for reducing their carbon footprints. If they somehow haven't, it will take five seconds on the internet to find advice. There are dozens of good books they could read, plenty of good documentaries. Perhaps I'm being unfair, but if people don't know very basic things about environmentally responsible living, I wonder if it's because they don't want to know. The idea that it's too confusing excuses people from taking action.

I don't accept this narrative that it's difficult. It's not. Children understand it, while adults throw their hands up and say they can't work it out. Perhaps it's not a conscious decision, but it is a choice nonetheless. Faced with a potentially existential crisis, many people have chosen to never read a book on it, watch a documentary or run a five-second Google search. They say it's all very confusing and so they have done nothing.

This is common. It's a very human response that psychologists have understood for a long time. In the English language it is called denial.

I see this at work in the race debate too. Whenever race is in the news, people turn to their Black friends or the person of colour in the office and ask what White people can do to support Black Lives Matter. Like the question about three simple things to reduce your carbon footprint, what the question accidentally reveals is two-fold. First, the person hasn't bothered to look into this for themselves on even a cursory level. Again, a five-second Google search will deliver the answers they claim to seek. Secondly, the question implies that the person of colour should teach White people about race, rather than the White person having a responsibility to educate themselves.

'During the COVID-19 pandemic, would you ask someone who is currently in the hospital healing from the coronavirus what you can do to avoid getting the virus?' asks the African-American writer Laura Adom. 'As Black people, it is not our responsibility to educate and teach you how to erase your racist views, especially not when we're currently working on our healing through these moments ourselves.'[5]

'People of colour are not obligated to teach even the most well-intentioned White people anything about race,' says the journalist Kali Holloway on similar lines. 'If you're a White person who wants to be an ally, who's dedicated to learning, who wants to be educated, start by *looking it up yourself*!'[6]

Listen, learn

At the start of this book, I mentioned that I was unsure whether I should attempt it or not. I knew the book was important, but I thought a person of colour should write it. Then I realised that this assumption made race into a Black issue, as if White people have no part in it. And I had plenty of personal experience of White privilege.

Another hesitation for me was having the language to talk about race. I've been writing about environmental issues for well over a decade and I feel fluent in that field. It took me a long time to find the right tone of voice for this book. I wrote and discarded far more material than usual. I have felt my way into the topic.

What has given me confidence is reading Black and minority ethnic writers, Asian, African, American, Indigenous, in both fiction and non-fiction. My own thoughts slowly crystallised, but only after years spent just listening. I cannot recommend it enough.

I wish I had been taught more about these things at school. I went to an American Christian boarding school in Kenya. Climate change was not on the curriculum. We never talked about race, despite an obvious hierarchy. (White expatriates filled all the teaching and managerial roles and were referred to as 'staff members'. Kenyans had jobs in the kitchens or the laundry and were called 'workers'.)

University didn't do much better, minus the identity politics covered in cultural studies lectures. I have had to do a lot of looking it up myself, and it took me far too long to realise that I needed to be proactive in going out and learning about race, rather than waiting for the information to come to me. As

I have learned, I have at times shuddered at views I have held or things I have said in the past. I will have made mistakes in this book, and I recognise that I'm not going to get everything right in future either. I intend to keep learning, keep listening, and only speak when I have something useful to say.

I never went to school in Britain or America and I can't comment on what most people learn. But I can see from the news that it is quite possible to ascend all the way to the upper echelons of government without ever understanding structural racism. You can be prime minister, two decades into the 21st century, and still think that the British Empire was a good thing and colonialism is all in the past. So it is vital that race is covered in education. Not just a token dip into Black History Month, or the bits that make White students feel good because their ancestors freed the slaves, but the full context of empire and privilege. I hope that my own children will be more aware of race and privilege than I have been, and more confident in confronting it.

Build empathy

In Chapter 8 I looked at the problem of compassion fatigue and the empathy gap. Education and dialogue can help to close this divide, along with greater representation of minority voices in all walks of life, and a commitment to learning and listening. Art, music and literature can break down divides. As a lover of books, I have enjoyed immersing myself in good fiction, seeing the world through the eyes of others – Colson Whitehead, Octavia

Butler, Pitchaya Sudbanthad, Esi Edugyan, N.K. Jemisin, Nana Kwame Adjei-Brenyah, to name a few.

Film can do this too. 'We are who we are: where we were born, who we were born as, how we were raised,' the film critic Roger Ebert once said. 'We're kind of stuck inside that person, and the purpose of civilization and growth is to be able to reach out and empathise a little bit with other people. And for me, the movies are like a machine that generates empathy. It lets you understand a little bit more about different hopes, aspirations, dreams and fears.'[7]

Black Panther, released in 2018, is one of the highest grossing films of all time, and one that raises prickly questions. The fictional kingdom of Wakanda was never colonised and has become the most technologically sophisticated nation on Earth – and a sustainable one too. It's a subversive political vision of what Africa might have been if it was not plundered by the colonists. Audiences clearly responded to a Black superhero, but the world had waited a long time for Black sci-fi too, for Afro-futurism in widescreen.

I showed my children the film *The Boy Who Harnessed the Wind*, the story of William Kamkwamba, a teenager from Malawi who brought electricity to his family with a home-made wind turbine. It's an entirely African story that deals with the realities of living with a changing climate. It is an entertainment product, but far from trivial. It is easy to hold race, poverty or climate justice at a mental distance as 'issues', as abstract problems to be solved. Storytelling helps to 'humanise' and personalise them, building empathy across difference. If Hollywood wants to affirm that Black lives matter, what better way than to let audiences in on Black lives?

This is particularly important for Africa, which is so under-represented in global politics and culture, and is therefore overlooked in the climate crisis. But Africa is not a problem. It is not a crisis, a tragedy or an unfulfilled promise. 'Africa is people,' writes the Nigerian novelist Chinua Achebe.[8]

Antiracism

As I try to live well as a White person in a structurally racist society, empathy and understanding are important start-ing points. But as Terri Givens describes in her book *Radical Empathy*, this isn't just a matter of being a nice person: under-standing another person's point of view should lead us into action on what matters to them. To really make a difference then, I have to push back against racism. Silence always protects privilege, so simply making sure that I am not personally part of the problem leaves racist structures intact. 'You don't have to be *a* racist to be racist,' writes the Nigerian journalist OluTimehin Adegbeye. 'It's racist to just passively allow racism to continue.'[9]

Ibram X. Kendi puts it well in his helpfully titled book *How to Be an Antiracist*: 'There is no neutrality in the racism strug-gle. The opposite of "racist" isn't "not racist". It is "antiracist."'[10]

Antiracism is not something that you are, but something you do. It is a constant series of choices, a lifelong struggle to expose and oppose the structures of racism. Because it is something you do, it isn't to do with colour – you can be a White antiracist, in the same way that a man can be a feminist. And power matters. Racism is embedded in ideas and policies, in political structures that serve elites. Tackling racist attitudes is helpful at the individual level, but it is only when racist power and policymaking are confronted that real systemic change happens.

Kehinde Andrews argues that 'the primary logic underpinning the Western world order is that Black and Brown life is worth less'.[11] Climate change is the biggest manifestation of this, and so as a climate change activist, I must also be an antiracist. As I seek to oppose racist power structures, I have to be a climate activist. These are not two issues. This is one story, one struggle.

Difficult questions

When I first began researching this book, I created a folder on my laptop and called it 'Is climate change racist?' It lost the question mark along the way, and you'll know that the answer to that initial question is yes – climate change is racist. It is racist in its origins and its effects, part of a White supremacist legacy that reaches deep into the past, through slavery, empire and neo-colonialism.

There is a continuity of oppression that runs from the enslaving of Black people for the benefit of White industrialisation, to the stealing of indigenous land for the enrichment of White empires, to the pollution of the atmosphere for the benefit of White consumerism. It is one story: the same people taking the plunder, the same people suffering.

Throughout that story, there have been those who have pushed the other way: the rebel slaves and the abolitionists, the satyagrahis who walked with Gandhi for Indian freedom, the campaigners for African independence, the civil rights marchers. Black Lives Matter and intersectional climate activism are part of this same tradition, still confronting the injustices of White entitlement to the land, resources and bodies of people of colour.

Where am I going to stand? Whose side am I on?

We each need to make our own responses, and you will need to decide what this moment calls you to. Where will you stand?

In this chapter, I have set out some of the things I am committed to. I am going to keep working to reduce my carbon footprint, personally and in my sphere of influence, in solidarity with those already suffering. I will keep advocating for clean energy and a just transition away from fossil fuels, and protesting the powers that oppose these steps forward. I will listen more than I speak. I will keep learning from people of colour, seeking out new perspectives and amplifying the voices of those who are marginalised. I will seek to be intersectional in my activism. I will be antiracist.

I will keep asking difficult questions.

Acknowledgements

Despite being a short book, this is one that has been a long time in the writing – or more to the point, the thinking. When it first occurred to me that climate change was racist, I had never heard anyone else say it. It was through the work of many writers and thinkers that I gradually began to understand and articulate this connection, and I am indebted to Robert D. Bullard, Beverly Wright, Dorceta Taylor and the pioneers of environmental justice. My thinking has also been shaped by Ha-Joon Chang, Jason Hickel, Kehinde Andrews, Kevin O'Brien, Ibram X. Kendi, Mary Robinson, Kimberlé Crenshaw, Ta-Nehisi Coates and many others.

Thank you to the climate justice writers, campaigners and advocates who showed me I was not alone in seeing a racial dimension to climate change, including Mary Annaïse Heglar, Leon Sealey Huggins, Ayana Elizabeth Johnson, Vanessa Nakate, Eric Holthaus, Leah Thomas, Mohamed Adow, Katharine K. Wilkinson, Asad Rehman, Jacqui Patterson, Emily Atkin.

Special thanks to Dario Kenner for his work on the carbon elite, D'Arcy Lunn for checking my Peace Studies, Augustine Njamnshi for his perspective on the Copenhagen climate talks, Nnimmo Bassey on neo-colonialism, and Samantha Lindo for being the first reader. Thank you to friends in Luton, in XR,

CCA and Tearfund who have supported the book and read early drafts.

The book would not be in your hands without my agent Laetitia Rutherford, who believed in it from the outset. Kiera Jamison has also been an enthusiast for the book, along with Hanna Milner, Hamza Jahanzeb and the team at Icon. Thank you to Dr Shola Mos-Shogbamimu for the foreword. Thank you to Marie Doherty for typesetting and to Martin Lubikowski for creating the figures.

Most of all, thank you to Lou, Zach and Eden, aka the staff and students of Hart Lane Academy. It's been a year to remember, and I'm glad I spent it with you.

Notes

Introduction

1. The Stephen Lawrence Inquiry, Report of an Inquiry by Sir William Macpherson of Cluny. Presented to Parliament February 1999. https://assets.publishing.service.gov.uk/government/uploads/system/uploads/attachment_data/file/277111/4262.pdf

2. *Black Power: The politics of liberation*, Kwame Ture (Stokely Carmichael) and Charles V. Hamilton, Random House, 1967, p4.

3. *The New Politics of Race: Globalism, Difference, Justice*, Howard Winant, University of Minnesota Press, 2004, p126.

4. *Systemic Racism: A Theory of Oppression*, Joe R. Feagin, Routledge, 2013, p11.

5. *Racism Without Racists: Colour-blind racism and the persistence of racial inequality in America*, Eduardo Bonilla-Silva, Rowman & Littlefield, 2010.

6. Christian Aid, Covid, Climate Change and Racism Poll. Savanta ComRes, Christian Aid, June 2020. https://comresglobal.com/polls/christian-aid-climate-justice-and-race/

7. 'Why Climate Change Is a Civil Rights Issue', Rev. Dr. Gerald Durley, *Huffington Post*, 30 August 2013. https://www.huffpost.com/entry/climate-change-civil-rights_b_3844986

8. *What We're Fighting for Now Is Each Other: Dispatches from the front lines of climate justice*, Wen Stephenson, Beacon Press, 2015, p31.

Chapter 1

1. *The God Species: How the planet can survive the age of humans*, Mark Lynas, Fourth Estate, 2011, p8.

2. *Ten Billion*, Stephen Emmott, Penguin, 2013, pp1–6.

3. Figures from CIA World Factbook, 2016, https://en.wikipedia.org/wiki/List_of_countries_by_electricity_consumption

4. William Catton at the 2011 conference of the Association for the Study of Peak Oil and Gas. https://grist.org/article/2011-11-04-each-american-consumes-as-much-energy-as-40-ton-dinosaur/

5. 'Fossil CO_2 emissions of all world countries', EDGAR, 2018. https://op.europa.eu/s/oSTB

6. 'Who has contributed most to carbon emissions?', Hannah Ritchie, *Our World in Data*, 2019. https://ourworldindata.org/contributed-most-global-co2

7. 'The Carbon Majors Database: CDP Carbon Majors Report 2017', Paul Griffin, CDP Worldwide, 2017.

8. Analysis for the *Guardian*, Richard Heede, Climate Accountability Institute, 2019.

9. 'The rise in global atmospheric CO_2, surface temperature, and sea level from emissions traced to major carbon producers', B. Ekwurzel et al., *Climatic Change*, Vol 144, 2017, pp 579–90.

10. 'Names and locations of the top 100 people killing the planet', Jordan Engel, The Decolonial Atlas, 27 April 2019. https://decolonialatlas.wordpress.com/2019/04/27/names-and-locations-of-the-top-100-people-killing-the-planet/

11. The Polluter Elite Database, compiled by Dario Kenner, is available to download from http://whygreeneconomy.org/

12. *Global Planet Authority*, Angus Forbes, LID Publishing Ltd, 2019, p42.

13. *Planet of Humans*, directed by Jeff Gibbs, YouTube, 2020.

14. *A Billion Black Anthropocenes or None*, Kathryn Yusoff, University of Minnesota Press, 2018.

15. See *The Shock of the Anthropocene*, Christophe Bonneuil and Jean-Baptiste Fressoz, Verso, 2017, p71.

16. Quoted in *Climate Justice: Hope, Resilience and the Fight for a Sustainable Future*, Mary Robinson, Bloomsbury Publishing, 2018, p17.

Chapter 2

1. *Reporting Disaster: Famine, Aid, Politics and the Media*, Suzanne Franks, Hurst Publishing, 2013, p25.

2. 'Tropical Rainfall Trends and the Indirect Aerosol Effect', Leon D. Rotstayn and Ulrike Lohmann, *Journal of Climate*, 15, January 2002, pp2103–16.

3. 'West's pollution led to African droughts', *BBC News*, 13 June 2002. http://news.bbc.co.uk/1/hi/world/africa/2042856.stm

4. *The Comforting Whirlwind*, Bill McKibben, Cowley Publications, 2005, p14.

5. 'Global mismatch between greenhouse gas emissions and the burden of climate change', G. Althor, J. Watson and R. Fuller, *Sci Rep*, 6, 20281, 2016. https://www.nature.com/articles/srep20281

6. '2 Degrees', Kathy Jetñil-Kijiner, July 2015. https://www.kathy jetnilkijiner.com/poem-2-degrees/

7. Acceptance speech for the Right Livelihood Award, Tony de Brum, 2015. https://www.rightlivelihoodaward.org/speech/acceptance-speech-tony-de-brum-the-people-of-the-marshall-islands/

8. 'Facing unbearable heat, Qatar has begun to air-condition the outdoors', Steven Mufson, *Washington Post*, 16 October 2019. https://www.washingtonpost.com/graphics/2019/world/climate-environment/climate-change-qatar-air-conditioning-outdoors/

9. 'Heatwave, advent of Ramazan leave roads deserted', Intikhab Hanif, *Dawn*, 29 May 2017. https://www.dawn.com/news/1336063/heatwave-advent-of-ramazan-leave-roads-deserted

10. *Global Climate Risk Index 2020*, David Eckstein, Vera Künzel, Laura Schäfer, Maik Winges. Germanwatch, December 2019.

11. 'Tropical Cyclones and Climate Change: An Indian Ocean Perspective', Thomas R. Knutson in *Indian Ocean Tropical Cyclones and Climate Change*, ed. Yassine Charabi, Springer, 2010.

12. *Managing the Risks of Extreme Events and Disasters to Advance Climate Change Adaptation*. Special Report of working groups 1 & 2 of the IPCC, ed. C.B. Field et al., Cambridge University Press, 2012, p582.

13. Christian Aid, Covid, Climate Change and Racism Poll.

14. 'Suffering in Silence: The 10 most under-reported humanitarian crises of 2019', CARE, January 2020. https://insights.careinternational. org.uk/publications/suffering-in-silence-the-10-most-under-reported-humanitarian-crises-of-2019

15. Ibid.

16. For a summary of Equiano's story and impact, see *Bury the Chains*, Adam Hochschild, Houghton Mifflin Harcourt, 2006, p169.

17. *Shock Waves: Managing the Impacts of Climate Change on Poverty*, Stephane Hallegatte et al., Climate Change and Development Series, World Bank, 2016.

18. *Turn Down the Heat: Climate Extremes, Regional Impacts, and the Case for Resilience*, World Bank, 2013, pxi.

19. 'Ethiopia switches on Africa's largest wind farm', Colin Barras, *New Scientist*, 29 October 2013. https://www.newscientist.com/ article/dn24485-ethiopia-switches-on-africas-largest-wind-farm/#ixzz6P4hQwKLI

20. As of June 2020, tracked by the Energy and Climate Intelligence Unit, https://eciu.net/netzerotracker/map

21. 'The Climate Crisis is a Racist Crisis: Structural racism, inequality and climate change', Leon Sealey-Huggins in *The Fire Now: Anti-racist scholarship in times of explicit racial violence*, ed. Azeezat Johnson, Remi Joseph-Salisbury and Beth Kamunge, Zed Books, 2018.

Chapter 3

1. 'Liam Hemsworth Is Back in Action', Scott Henderson, *Men's Health*, 13 April 2020.

2. 'The unequal vulnerability of communities of color to wildfire', Ian P. Davies, Ryan D. Haugo, James C. Robertson, Phillip S. Levin, *PLOS One*, 2 November 2018. https://doi.org/10.1371/journal. pone.0205825

3. 'Inequalities, inequities, environmental justice in waste management and health', M. Martuzzi, F. Mitis and F. Forastiere, *European Journal of Public Health*, Vol 20(1), 2010, pp21–6.

4. 'Racial Inequality in the Distribution of Hazardous Waste: A National Level Reassessment', P. Mohai and R. Saha, *Social Problems*, Vol 54(3), 2007, pp343–70.

5. *Dumping in Dixie: Race, class and environmental quality*, Robert D. Bullard, Westview Press, 1990, Preface, pxv.

6. Quoted in *What We're Fighting for Now Is Each Other: Dispatches from the front lines of climate justice*, Wen Stephenson, Beacon Press, 2015, p79.

7. 'Environmental Injustice in France', L. Laurien, *Journal of Environmental Planning and Management*, Vol 51(1), 2008, pp55–79.

8. 'Environmental Justice and Roma Communities in Central and Eastern Europe', K. Harper, T. Steger and R. Filcak, *Environmental Policy and Governance*, 5, 2009.

9. 'Lac-Megantic: The runaway train that destroyed a town', Jessica Murphy, *BBC News*, 19 January 2018.

10. *Environmental Justice and Oil Trains in Pennsylvania*, ACTION United, ForestEthics & PennEnvironment Research & Policy Center, February 2016. https://pennenvironment.org/sites/environment/files/reports/OilTrainPAReport_r1.pdf

11. This story is told in *Against Doom: A Climate Insurgency Manual*, Jeremy Brecher, PM Press, 2017.

12. Quoted in *Standing Rock: Greed, Oil and the Lakota Struggle for Justice*, Bikem Ekberzade, Zed Books, 2018, p41.

13. 'Standing Rock Sioux Tribe Wins a Victory in Dakota Access Pipeline Case', Lisa Friedman, *The New York Times*, 25 March 2020. https://www.nytimes.com/2020/03/25/climate/dakota-access-pipeline-sioux.html

14. *This Changes Everything: Capitalism vs the Climate*, Naomi Klein, Allen Lane, 2014, p310.

15. *The Toxic Truth*, Amnesty International & Greenpeace, 2012. https://www.greenpeace.org/archive-international/Global/international/publications/toxics/ProboKoala/The-Toxic-Truth.pdf

16. *War on Plastic with Hugh and Anita*, screened on BBC 1, June 2019.

17. *Discarded: Communities on the frontlines of the global plastic crisis*, GAIA, 2019. https://wastetradestories.org/wp-content/uploads/2019/04/Discarded-Report-April-22.pdf

18. *Voices from the Storm: The People of New Orleans on Hurricane Katrina and its Aftermath*, ed. Lola Vollen and Chris Ying, McSweeney's, 2015.

19. See *The Wrong Complexion for Protection: How the government response to disaster endangers African American communities*, Robert D. Bullard and Beverly Wright, New York University Press, 2012.

20. Cited in 'A Tale of Three Cities', Jainey K. Bavishi, in *All We Can Save*, ed. Ayana Elizabeth Johnson and Katharine K. Wilkinson, OneWorld, 2020, p157.

21. 'Liberty City Residents Worry They're Being Poisoned by Huge Hurricane Irma Dumpsite', Isabella Vi Gomes, *Miami New Times*, 3 November 2017. https://www.miaminewtimes.com/news/miami-dade-dumps-hurricane-debris-in-liberty-city-9798918

22. 'Impact, efficiency, inequality and injustice of urban air pollution: variability by emission location', Nam P. Nguyen and Julian D. Marshall, *Environmental Research Letters*, Vol 13(2), 2018.

23. 'Pennsylvania's children face lead perils everywhere', Wendy Ruderman and Barbara Laker, *Philadelphia Enquirer*, 7 June 2019. https://www.inquirer.com/news/toxic-city-lead-poisoning-children-philadelphia-schools-asbestos-20190607.html

24. 'Robert Bullard: "Environmental justice isn't just slang, it's real"', interview with Oliver Milman, the *Guardian*, 20 December 2018.

25. Alexandria Ocasio-Cortez, interviewed by Amy Goodman, *Democracy Now!*, 7 April 2020. https://www.democracynow.org/2020/4/7/aoc_coronavirus_queens_bronx

26. *Racism Without Racists: Color-blind racism and the persistence of racial inequality in America*, Eduardo Bonilla-Silva, Rowman & Littlefield, 2010, p8.

27. *How to Be an Antiracist*, Ibram X. Kendi, The Bodley Head, 2019, p230.

Chapter 4

1. Grace is fictionalised, but based on a case study from Practical Action.

2. *I Know Why the Caged Bird Sings*, Maya Angelou, Virago Press, 1984, p265.

3. *Intersectionality: Origins, Contestations, Horizons*, Anna Carastathis, University of Nebraska Press, 2016.

4. 'The Urgency of Intersectionality', talk given by Kimberlé Crenshaw to the TED Conference, October 2016. https://www.ted.com/talks/kimberle_crenshaw_the_urgency_of_intersectionality/transcript

5. *Gender Differences in Poverty and Household Composition through the Life-cycle: A Global Perspective*, Ana Maria Munoz Boudet et al., Policy Research Working Paper 8360, World Bank, 2018. http://documents.worldbank.org/curated/en/135731520343670750/pdf/WPS8360.pdf

6. Facts and Figures, UN Women, 2012. https://www.unwomen.org/en/news/in-focus/commission-on-the-status-of-women-2012/facts-and-figures

7. 'Progress on the Sustainable Development Goals: The Gender Snapshot 2019', UN Women, 2019. https://www.unwomen.org/en/digital-library/publications/2019/09/progress-on-the-sustainable-development-goals-the-gender-snapshot-2019

8. 'The gendered nature of natural disasters: the impact of catastrophic events on the gender gap in life expectancy, 1981–2002', Eric Neumayer and Thomas Plümper, *Annals of the Association of American Geographers*, Vol. 97(3), 2007, pp 551–66.

9. *Drawdown: The Most Comprehensive Plan Ever Proposed to Reverse Global Warming*, ed. Paul Hawken, Penguin Books, 2017.

10. *The Right to be Cold*, Sheila Watt Cloutier, University of Minnesota Press, 2015, p323.

11. *Turning Back to The Sea*, F. Balata and O. Vardakoulias, New Economics Foundation, 2016.

12. 'Climate change in Kenya: if we don't act now, we Turkana could lose our homes', Ekai Nabenyo, the *Guardian*, 9 November 2015.

13. 'An Appeal to the Church', Francesca Laven, in *Time to Act: A Resource Book from the Christians in Extinction Rebellion*, ed. Jeremy Williams, SPCK, 2020, p30.

14. *Heat Wave: A Social Autopsy of Disaster in Chicago*, Eric Klinenberg, University of Chicago Press, 2015, p17.

15. 'Bushfire smoke, pollution responsible for over 400 excess deaths', Isabelle Dubach, University of New South Wales press release, 23 March 2020.

16. See *#FutureGen: Lessons from a Small Country*, Jane Davidson, Chelsea Green Publishing, 2020.

Chapter 5

1. See *The Human Planet: How We Created the Anthropocene*, Simon L. Lewis and Mark A. Maslin, Pelican, 2018.

2. 'Climate change isn't racist – people are', Mary Annaïse Heglar, *Zora*, 13 August 2019. https://zora.medium.com/climate-change-isnt-racist-people-are-c586b9380965

3. Slave Trade Abolition Bill, 23 February 1807, *Hansard*, Vol. 8 and 16 March 1807, *Hansard*, Vol. 9. https://hansard.parliament.uk

4. *Bury the Chains*, Adam Hochschild, Houghton Mifflin Harcourt, 2006, p314.

5. Cited in *Rule Britannia: Brexit and the end of Empire*, Danny Dorling and Sally Tomlinson, Biteback Books, 2019, p124.

6. *The Descent of Man*, Charles Darwin, John Murray, 1871, pp388, 394.

7. *The Myth of Equality: Uncovering the Roots of Injustice and Privilege*, Ken Wytsma, IVP Books, 2017, p40.

8. Cited in *Toussaint Louverture: A Black Jacobin in the Age of Revolutions*, Charles Forsdick and Christian Høgsbjerg, Pluto Press, 2017, p37.

9. *Legacies of British Slave Ownership*, UCL. https://www.ucl.ac.uk/lbs/

10. 'Bedfordshire and the Slave Trade', Bedfordshire Archives and Records Service. http://bedsarchives.bedford.gov.uk/Newsletters/BedfordshireandtheSlaveTrade.aspx

11. Ibid., also *The Anti-Slavery Reporter*, Zachary Macaulay, Vol. 4, 1831, p69.

12. *Capitalism and Slavery*, Eric Williams, University of North Carolina edition, 2014, p102.

13. *Between the World And Me*, Ta-Nehisi Coates, Text Publishing, 2015, p70.

14. *The Divide: A Brief Guide to Global Inequality and its Solutions*, Jason Hickel, Windmill Books, 2017, p74.

15. *The New Age of Empire*, Kehinde Andrews, Allen Lane, 2021, p75.

16. Cited in *Hatred for Black People*, Shehu Sani, Xlibris, 2013, p107.

17. *Neo-colonialism: The Last Stage of Imperialism*, Kwame Nkrumah, Nelson, 1965.

18. *Safe for Democracy: The Secret Wars of the CIA*, John Prados, Rowman & Littlefield, 2006, p330.

19. *How Europe Underdeveloped Africa*, Walter Rodney, East African Publishers, 1972, p22.

20. *Poverty and Famines: An essay on entitlement and deprivation*, Amartya Sen, OUP, 1981, 2013, p15.

21. *Dead Aid*, Dambisa Moyo, Farrar, Straus & Giroux, 2010.

22. *Kicking Away the Ladder*, Ha-Joon Chang, Anthem Press, 2003, p2.

23. *To Cook a Continent: Destructive Extraction and the Climate Crisis in Africa*, Nnimmo Bassey, Pambazuka Press, 2012, p36.

24. *Ecological Debt: Global Warming and the Wealth of Nations*, Andrew Simms, Pluto Press, 2009, p88.

25. *Laudato Si': On Care for Our Common Home*, Pope Francis, 2015, Chapter 1, paragraph 52.

26. 'The British Empire is "something to be proud of"', Will Dahlgreen, YouGov, 2014. https://yougov.co.uk/topics/politics/articles-reports/2014/07/26/britain-proud-its-empire

27. 'Africa is a mess, but we can't blame colonialism', Boris Johnson, *Spectator*, 14 July 2016. https://www.spectator.co.uk/article/the-boris-archive-africa-is-a-mess-but-we-can-t-blame-colonialism

28. 'The future of climate activism must centre people of colour', Janine Francois, *Huffington Post*, 2 May 2019.

29. 'This Monstrous Shadow: Race, climate and justice', Anthony Reddie, in *Time to Act*, ed. Jeremy Williams, SPCK, 2020, pp75, 76.

Chapter 6

1. The Count: Police Killings Database, the *Guardian*, 2015. https://www.theguardian.com/us-news/ng-interactive/2015/jun/01/the-counted-police-killings-us-database

2. 'Here's How Many Cops Got Convicted of Murder Last Year for On-Duty Shootings', Matt Ferner and Nick Wing, *Huffington Post*, 31 January 2016.

3. 'Cleveland officer who fatally shot Tamir Rice will not face criminal charges', Oliver Laughland, Jon Swaine and Daniel McGraw, the *Guardian*, 28 December 2015. https://www.theguardian.com/us-news/2015/dec/28/tamir-rice-shooting-no-charges-cleveland-officer-timothy-loehmann

4. 'The gap between the number of blacks and whites in prison is shrinking', John Gramlich, Pew Research Center, *Fact Tank*, 30 April 2019. https://pewrsr.ch/2J66aNq

5. 'Letter from a Birmingham Jail', Martin Luther King, Jr., 1963, The Martin Luther King, Jr. Research and Education Institute, Stanford University. https://kinginstitute.stanford.edu/king-papers/documents/letter-birmingham-jail

6. 'Regional Ethnic Diversity', Office for National Statistics, 2018. https://www.ethnicity-facts-figures.service.gov.uk/uk-population-by-ethnicity/national-and-regional-populations/regional-ethnic-diversity/latest

7. 'Black Lives Matter protesters close London City Airport runway', *BBC News*, 6 September 2016. https://www.bbc.co.uk/news/uk-england-london-37283869

8. 'The children of privilege who loathe the system that gave them every advantage: The truth about the (white) Black Lives Matter protesters who closed London City airport', Guy Adams, *Daily Mail*, 16 September 2016. https://www.dailymail.co.uk/news/article-3793611/The-children-privilege-loathe-gave-advantage-truth-white-Black-Lives-Matter-protesters-closed-London-City-airport-ll-want-protest-against-THEM.html

9. 'Climate change is a racist crisis: that's why Black Lives Matter closed an airport', Alexandra Wanjiku Kelbert, the *Guardian*, 6 September 2016. https://www.theguardian.com/commentisfree/2016/sep/06/climate-change-racist-crisis-london-city-airport-black-lives-matter

10. 'Ella Kissi-Debrah inquest: Coroner says air pollution contributed to death of nine-year-old in landmark ruling', Harry Cockburn, the *Independent*, 16 December 2020.

11. 'London's black communities disproportionately exposed to air pollution – study', Adam Vaughn, the *Guardian*, 10 October 2016.

12. *Johan Galtung: Pioneer of Peace Research*, Johan Galtung and Dietrich Fischer. Springer-Verlag, 29 May 2013, pp12, 46.

13. *The Wrong Complexion for Protection: How the government response to disaster endangers African American communities*, Robert D. Bullard and Beverly Wright, New York University Press, 2012.

14. *Dried up, Drowned out: Voices from poor communities on a changing climate*, Tearfund, 2012, p11.

15. *Slow violence and the environmentalism of the poor*, Rob Nixon, Harvard University Press, 2011, p2.

16. *The Violence of Climate Change: Lessons of resistance from nonviolent activists*, Kevin J. O'Brien, Georgetown University Press, 2017, p2.

17. 'Black Environmentalists Talk About Climate and Anti-Racism', Somini Sengupta, *The New York Times*, 3 June 2020.

18. 'Climate justice through Pan-Afrikan Reparatory justice', Kofi Mawuli Klu and Esther Stanford-Xosei, Open Democracy,

3 December 2015. https://www.opendemocracy.net/en/climate-justice-through-pan-afrikan-reparator/

19. 'In Germany's extermination program for Black Africans, a template for the Holocaust', Edwin Black, *Times of Israel*, 5 May 2016. https://www.timesofisrael.com/in-germanys-extermination-program-for-black-africans-a-template-for-the-holocaust/

20. 'Maangamizi', Akala, on *The Thieves Banquet*, Illa State Records, 2013.

21. 'Crisis for Republican party as Trump heads for Super Tuesday victory', David Smith, Ben Jacobs and Sabrina Siddiqui, the *Guardian*, 1 March 2016. https://www.theguardian.com/us-news/2016/mar/01/super-tuesday-crisis-republican-party-trump-heads-for-victory

Chapter 7

1. Matt Ridley in conversation with Roger Harrabin, *Changing Climate*, BBC Radio 4, 13 November 2015. Transcript available from Open University. https://www.open.edu/openlearn/nature-environment/the-environment/creative-climate/stories-change/matt-ridley-stories-change?in_menu=322619

2. 'On the Influence of Carbonic Acid in the Air upon the Temperature of the Ground', Svante Arrhenius, *The London, Edinburgh, and Dublin Philosophical Magazine and Journal of Science*, Vol. 41, April 1896, pp237–76.

3. Good summaries of the early years of climate science can be found in *The Shock of the Anthropocene*, by Christophe Bonneuil and Jean-Baptiste Fressoz, and *The Human Planet*, by Simon Lewis and Mark Maslin.

4. CO_2 Greenhouse Effect, briefing paper, Exxon Research and Engineering Company, 12 November 1982. http://www.climatefiles.com/exxonmobil/1982-memo-to-exxon-management-about-co2-greenhouse-effect/

5. 'The conduct of Viscount Ridley', report to the House by the Committee for Privileges and Conduct, January 2014. https://publications.parliament.uk/pa/ld201314/ldselect/ldprivi/119/11903.htm

6. *Diversifying Power: Why we need Antiracist, Feminist Leadership on Climate and Energy,* Jennie C Stephens, Island Press, 2020, p13.

7. 'Climate policies are doing more harm than good – a moral issue', Matt Ridley, in *Climate Change: The Facts 2017*, ed. Jennifer Marohasy, Connor Court Publishing, 2017.

8. 'James Murdoch Slams Fox News and News Corp Over Climate-Change Denial', Lachlan Cartwright, *Daily Beast*, 14 January 2020. https://www.thedailybeast.com/james-murdoch-slams-fox-news-and-news-corp-over-climate-change-denial

9. 'The spillover of race and racial attitudes into public opinion about climate change', Salil D. Benegal, *Environmental Politics*, Vol. 27(4), 2018, pp733–56.

10. 'Which racial/ethnic groups care most about climate change?', M. Ballew et al., Yale University and George Mason University, Yale Program on Climate Change Communication, 2020. https://climatecommunication.yale.edu/publications/race-and-climate-change/

11. Quoted in *Don't Even Think About It*, George Marshall, Bloomsbury, 2014, p82.

12. 'Climate Denial and the Construction of Innocence: Re-Producing Transnational Environmental Privilege in the Face of Climate Change' Kari Marie Norgaard, *Race, Gender & Class*, Vol. 19(1–2), 2012, pp80–103.

13. *Climate Change Denial,* Haydn Washington and John Cook, Earthscan, 2011, p2.

14. Cited in *The Myth of Equality: Uncovering the roots of Injustice and Privilege*, Ken Wytsma, IVP Books, 2017, p5.

15. *Why I'm no Longer Talking to White People About Race*, Reni Eddo-Lodge, Bloomsbury, 2018, p86.

16. 'For Our White Friends Desiring to Be Allies', Courtney Ariel, *Sojourners*, 16 August 2017.

Chapter 8

1. 'Ebola – as seen through the eyes of a 13-year-old from Sierra Leone', Bintu Sannoh, the *Guardian*, 11 October 2014.

2. 'A Short History of an Ebola Vaccine', Emmanuel Freudenthal, *The New Humanitarian*, 4 June 2019. https://www.thenewhumanitarian. org/analysis/2019/06/04/short-history-ebola-vaccine

3. 'First Ebola Case Diagnosed in the U.S.', Dina Fine Maron, *Scientific American*, 30 September 2014. https://www.scientificamerican.com/ article/first-ebola-case-diagnosed-in-the-u-s/

4. 'Newlink shares jump on start of Ebola vaccine study', Wallace Witkowski, *MarketWatch*, 13 October 2014. https://www.market watch.com/story/newlink-shares-jump-on-start-of-ebola-vaccine-study-2014-10-13

5. 'World Scientists Near Consensus on Warming', James Kanter and Andrew C. Revkin, *The New York Times*, 30 January 2007. https:// www.nytimes.com/2007/01/30/world/30climate.html

6. 'Hajj could become lethal if the climate crisis continues', press release, Islamic Relief, 29 August 2019. https://www.islamic-relief.org.uk/ hajj-could-become-lethal-if-the-climate-crisis-continues/

7. *Lander's Travels in Africa*, quoted in *The Negroes in Negroland: The Negroes in America; and Negroes Generally. Also, the Several Races of White Men, Considered as the Involuntary and Predestined Supplanters of the Black Races. A Compilation*, Hinton Rowan Helper, G. W. Carleton, 1868, p92.

8. 'Racial bias in pain assessment and treatment recommendations, and false beliefs about biological differences between Blacks and Whites', Kelly M. Hoffman, Sophie Trawalter, Jordan R. Axt, and M. Norman Oliver, *Proc Natl Acad Sci USA*, 113(16), 19 April 2016, pp4296–301. https://www.ncbi.nlm.nih.gov/pmc/articles/PMC4843483/

9. Ibid.

10. 'Racism and the Empathy for Pain on Our Skin', Matteo Forgiarini, Marcello Gallucci and Angelo Maravita, Front Psychol. 2011; 2: 108. https://www.ncbi.nlm.nih.gov/pmc/articles/PMC3108582/

11. 'Racial Bias in Perceptions of Others' Pain', Sophie Trawalter, Kelly M. Hoffman, Adam Waytz, *PLOS One*, 14 November 2012. https://doi.org/10.1371/journal.pone.0048546

12. Daviz Simango at Resilient Cities 2016, ICLEI – Local Governments for Sustainability, 22 July 2016. https://www.youtube.com/watch?v=djg2vGylGtg

13. 'Working on the ground' – Beira mayor Daviz Simango in first interview after cyclone, Club of Mozambique, 21 March 2019. https://clubofmozambique.com/news/working-on-the-ground-beira-mayor-daviz-simango-in-first-interview-after-cyclone/

14. CNN's top 100 digital stories of 2019, CNN Staff, 23 December 2019. https://edition.cnn.com/2019/12/22/us/top-100-digital-stories-2019-trnd/index.html

15. *Suffering in Silence: The 10 most under-reported humanitarian crises of 2019*, CARE International, January 2020.

16. YouGov, 2014. http://cdn.yougov.com/cumulus_uploads/document/6quatmbimd/Internal_Results_140725_Commonwealth_Empire-W.pdf

17. *Our House is on Fire*, Malena and Beata Ernman, Svante and Greta Thunberg, Allen Lane, London, 2020, p106.

18. *Leave the World Behind*, Rumaan Alam, Bloomsbury, 2020, p218.

19. *The New Age of Empire*, Kehinde Andrews, Allen Lane, 2021, p99.

20. 'Racial Bias in Perceptions of Others' Pain', Sophie Trawalter, Kelly M. Hoffman, Adam Waytz, *PLOS One*, 14 November 2012. https://doi.org/10.1371/journal.pone.0048546

21. *Radical Empathy: Finding a Path to Bridging Racial Divides*, Terri Givens, Policy Press, 2021, p55.

22. *Empathy: Why it Matters, And How to Get It*, Roman Krznaric, Ebury Publishing, 2015, p193.

Chapter 9

1. 'Central Park incident highlights "daily dangers in outdoor spaces" for African Americans', Matt Mendenhall, *Bird Watching Daily*, 26 May

2020. https://www.birdwatchingdaily.com/news/birdwatching/central-park-incident-highlights-daily-dangers-outdoor-spaces-african-americans/

2. '5 Key Lessons To Take Home From the First #BlackBirdersWeek', Gustave Axelson, 6 June 2020. https://www.allaboutbirds.org/news/5-key-lessons-to-take-home-from-the-first-blackbirdersweek/

3. *The Home Place: Memoirs of a Coloured Man's Love Affair with Nature*, J. Drew Lanham, Milkweed Editions, 2016.

4. '"Black Women Who Bird" Take the Spotlight to Make Their Presence Known', Tara Santora, *Audubon*, 5 June 2020. https://www.audubon.org/news/black-women-who-bird-take-spotlight-make-their-presence-known

5. 'Racial and Ethnic Differences in Connectedness to Nature and Landscape Preferences Among College Students,' Dorceta E. Taylor, *Environmental Justice*, April 2018.

6. Dudley Edmondson, speaking to Phoebe Judge on the podcast *This is Love*, Episode 22: 'Prairie Warbler', 13 May 2020. https://thisislovepodcast.com/episode-22-prairie-warbler

7. Cited in 'Minority Environmental Activism in Britain: From Brixton to the Lake District', Dorceta E. Taylor, *Qualitative Sociology*, Vol. 16(3), 1993.

8. See www.ingridpollard.com/pastoral-interlude.html

9. *The Great Derangement: Climate Change and the Unthinkable*, Amitav Ghosh, University of Chicago Press, 2016, p91.

10. Ibid, 107.

11. Ibid, 92.

12. 'Negotiating Who Lives and Dies: An interview with Asad Rehman about the crisis of our times', Demand Climate Justice, 7 March 2017. https://worldat1c.org/negotiating-who-lives-and-dies-5d400021b860

13. Ibid.

14. https://www.wwf.org.uk/get-involved/schools/resources/climate-change-resources (accessed 18 June 2020).

15. 'Mary Annaïse Heglar on why climate action is limitless', Yessenia Funes, *Atmos*, 2021. https://atmos.earth/mary-heglar-climate-change-intersectionality/

16. 'I'm a Black climate expert. Racism derails our efforts to save the planet', Ayana Elizabeth Johnson, *The Washington Post*, 3 June 2020. https://www.washingtonpost.com/outlook/2020/06/03/im-black-climate-scientist-racism-derails-our-efforts-save-planet/

Chapter 10

1. 'Climate change will hit Africa hardest', Meles Zenawi, the *Guardian*, 28 November 2009. https://www.theguardian.com/commentisfree/cif-green/2009/nov/28/africa-climate-change

2. 'Africa to Demand Legally-Binding Reparations at Climate Summit', *VoA*, 2 November 2009. https://www.voanews.com/archive/africa-demand-legally-binding-reparations-climate-summit

3. 'Climate change will hit Africa hardest', Meles Zenawi, the *Guardian*, 28 November 2009.

4. 'Sarkozy, Obama pressure Meles Zenawi to betray Africa at Copenhagen Talks', Jamie Henn, Ethiomedia, 16 December 2009. https://ethiomedia.com/course/4651.html

5. 'WikiLeaks cables reveal how US manipulated climate accord', Damian Carrington, the *Guardian*, 3 December 2010. https://www.theguardian.com/environment/2010/dec/03/wikileaks-us-manipulated-climate-accord

6. SUBJECT: DEPUTY NSA MICHAEL FROMAN VISIT TO BRUSSELS, JANUARY 27, 2010, Wikileaks. https://wikileaks.org/plusd/cables/10BRUSSELS183_a.html

7. UNDER SECRETARY OTERO'S MEETING WITH ETHIOPIAN PRIME MINISTER MELES ZENAWI – JANUARY 31, 2010, Wikileaks. https://wikileaks.org/plusd/cables/10ADDISABABA163_a.html

8. *The Climate Debt: What the West Owes the Rest*, Mohamed Adow, Foreign Affairs, May/June 2020, p60.

9. Paris Agreement, UNFCC, 2015. http://unfccc.int/files/essential_background/convention/application/pdf/english_paris_agreement.pdf

10. www.climateactiontracker.org (accessed 3 July 2020).

11. *How to Be an Antiracist*, Ibram X. Kendi, Random House Publishing Group, 2019, p21.

12. 'Statement and Proposal For Full Black American Reparations'. Press release on behalf of Robert L. Johnson, issued by The RJL Companies, 1 June 2020. https://www.prnewswire.com/news-releases/robert-l-johnson-founder-of-black-entertainment-television-and-the-rlj-companies-issues-statement-and-proposal-for-full-black-american-reparations-301068343.html

13. Malcolm X, TV interview, March 1964. Widely available online.

14. Research by Utsa Patnaik, cited in 'How Britain stole $45 trillion from India', Jason Hickel, *Al Jazeera*, 19 December 2018. https://www.aljazeera.com/indepth/opinion/britain-stole-45-trillion-india-181206124830851.html

15. Dr Shashi Tharoor MP – 'Britain Does Owe Reparations', Debate at the Oxford Union Society, 14 July 2015. Transcript available at https://singjupost.com/dr-shashi-tharoor-britain-does-owe-reparations-full-transcript/?singlepage=1

16. 'Jamaica calls for Britain to pay billions in slavery reparations as David Cameron makes first state visit', Adam Withnall, the *Independent*, 29 September 2015. https://www.independent.co.uk/news/world/americas/jamaica-calls-for-britain-to-pay-billions-in-slavery-reparations-as-david-cameron-makes-first-state-a6671346.html

17. Ibid.

18. 'Pub chain and insurance hub "sorry" for slave links', *BBC News*, 18 June 2020. https://www.bbc.co.uk/news/business-53087790

19. 'Africa' chapter, Niang, I., O.C. Ruppel et al., in *Climate Change 2014: Impacts, Adaptation, and Vulnerability. Part B: Regional Aspects*. Fifth Assessment Report of the Intergovernmental Panel on Climate Change. Cambridge University Press,Cambridge, United Kingdom and New York, USA, pp1199–265.

20. *Necropolitics*, Achille Mbembe, Duke University Press, 2019.

21. *The Little Book of Race and Restorative Justice: Black Lives, Healing, and US Social Transformation*, Fania E. Davis, Good Books, New York, 2019. (Ebook edition)

22. *Restorative Justice*, Ruth Ann Strickland, Peter Lang, 2004, p2.

23. 'The Case for Reparations', Ta-Nehisi Coates, *The Atlantic*, June 2014. https://www.theatlantic.com/magazine/archive/2014/06/the-case-for-reparations/361631/

Chapter 11

1. 'For the love of... what exactly?', Adam Corner, Climate Outreach, 10 October 2014. https://climateoutreach.org/love-of-what/

2. Open Letter from the Wretched of the Earth bloc to the organisers of the People's Climate March of Justice and Jobs, Reclaim the Power, 17 January 2016. https://reclaimthepower.org.uk/news/open-letter-from-wretched-of-the-earth-bloc-to-organisers-of-peoples-climate-march/

3. 'Darkening the White Heart of the Climate Movement', Alexandra Wanjiku Kelbert and Joshua Virasami, *New Internationalist*, 1 December 2015. https://newint.org/blog/guests/2015/12/01/darkening-the-white-heart-of-the-climate-movement/

4. 'Collards are just as good as kale', Heather McTeer Toney, in *All We Can Save*, ed. Ayana Elizabeth Johnson and Katharine K. Wilkinson, OneWorld, 2020, p157.

5. *Time to Act: A Resource Book from the Christians in Extinction Rebellion*, ed. Jeremy Williams, SPCK, 2020, p142.

6. 'The flawed social science behind Extinction Rebellion's change strategy', Nafeez Ahmed, *Medium*, 28 October 2019. https://medium.com/insurge-intelligence/the-flawed-science-behind-extinction-rebellions-change-strategy-af077b9abb4d

7. 'The Climate Justice Movement Must Oppose White Supremacy Everywhere', Mattias Lehman, Sunrise Movement Digital Director, Sunrise Movement, *Medium*, 29 May 2020. https://medium.com/sunrisemvmt/the-climate-justice-movement-must-

oppose-white-supremacy-everywhere-by-supporting-m4bl-4e338cf91b19

8. H. RES. 109, 'Recognizing the duty of the Federal Government to create a Green New Deal'. 116th CONGRESS, 1st Session, 2 July 2019. https://www.congress.gov/bill/116th-congress/house-resolution/109/text

9. https://www.sunrisemovement.org/ (accessed 1 July 2020).

10. 'Why Every Environmentalist Should Be Anti-Racist', Leah Thomas, *Vogue*, 8 June 2020. https://www.vogue.com/article/why-every-environmentalist-should-be-anti-racist

11. 'It's time to give white, working class boys a fair shot in life', Ben Bradley, *Politics Home*, 12 February 2020.

12. Forsdick and Hogsberg, 2017, p55.

13. 'William Cuffay: The Chartists' Black Leader', Tom Scriven, *Tribune*, 4 July 2020.

14. 'FACT SHEET: President Biden Takes Executive Actions to Tackle the Climate Crisis', The White House, 27 January 2021. https://www.whitehouse.gov/briefing-room/statements-releases/

15. Leah Thomas, https://www.intersectionalenvironmentalist.com/black

Chapter 12

1. 'Floods in India's Assam force a million from their homes', *Reuters*, 29 June 2020. https://www.reuters.com/article/us-india-floods/floods-in-indias-assam-force-a-million-from-their-homes-idUSKBN2400W0

2. '"Everything is lost": Life on the edge of the Brahmaputra', *The New Indian Express*, 13 January 2020. https://www.newindianexpress.com/nation/2020/jan/13/everything-is-lost-life-on-the-edge-of-the-brahmaputra-2089073.html

3. *The Uninhabitable Earth*, David Wallace-Wells, Allen Lane, 2019, p34.

4. *The Violence of Climate Change: Lessons of resistance from nonviolent activists*, Kevin J. O'Brien, Georgetown University Press, 2017, p181.

5. 'Please Don't Ask Your Black Friends to Teach You About Racism', Laura Adom, TheEveryMom, 10 June 2020. https://theeverymom.com/dont-ask-your-black-friends-to-teach-you-about-racism/

6. 'Black people are not here to teach you', Kali Holloway, *Salon*, 14 April 2015.

7. This is a favourite quote of the film critic Mark Kermode (hello to Jason Isaacs). 'Moving through empathy', Olivia Collette, RogerEbert.com, 27 January 2014. https://www.rogerebert.com/features/moving-through-empathy-on-life-itself

8. *Africa's Tarnished Name*, Chinua Achebe, Penguin, 2018, pp32, 40.

9. 'What racism really is', Olutimehin Adegbeye, *The Correspondent*, 24 June 2020, https://thecorrespondent.com/547/what-racism-really-is-hint-its-not-your-attitude-or-belief/

10. *How to Be an Antiracist*, Ibram X. Kendi, Random House Publishing Group, 2019, p9.

11. *The New Age of Empire*, Kehinde Andrews, Allen Lane, 2021, pix.